Clear & Simple
Crockery
Cooking:

RECIPES & INSTRUCTIONS FOR SLOW ELECTRIC COOKWARE
BY JACQUELINE HÉRITEAU

GROSSET
GOOD LIFE
BOOKS

PUBLISHERS · GROSSET & DUNLAP · NEW YORK

Acknowledgments

Many thanks to Kate Alfriend and Betty Fleming of the U.S.D.A. for supplying information on safe temperatures for food storage; to Walter Fischman, Francesca Bosetti Morris, Kerry Fitzgerald, and other friends for their slow-cooking recipes; and to Lee Schryver, Good Life editor, for his help in planning and illustrating this book. To Anne Le Moyne, thanks for difficult typing chores well done.

Cover photograph by Mort Engel

In addition, my thanks and appreciation to the following for their permission to use the photographs in this book: Better Foods, Inc., p. 51, p. 87, p. 88; Dudley-Anderson-Yutzy, Inc., p. 32, p. 34, p. 35 left, p. 47, p. 76; Evaporated Milk Association, p. 37 top, p. 78 top, p. 79; Bernard L. Lewis, Inc., p. 6; Lewis/Neale, Inc., p. 33; Frank Lusk, p. 12 bottom, p. 13 top, p. 17 top, p. 17 bottom, p. 18, p. 19 top, p. 19 bottom, p. 23, p. 27 top left, p. 27 top right, p. 27 bottom left, p. 27 bottom right, p. 37 right, p. 48, p. 49, p. 57 top, p. 57 bottom, p. 72 right, p. 73 top, p. 73 middle, p. 73 bottom, p. 83 top left, p. 83 top right, p. 83 bottom left, p. 83 bottom right, p. 84 top left, p. 84 top right, p. 84 bottom; Manning, Selvage and Lee, p. 38; National Canners Association, p. 30, p. 36 right, p. 63, p. 67, p. 72 left; National Live Stock & Meat Board, p. 31, p. 35 right, p. 64 left; National Pork Producers Council, p. 42; Oscar Mayer and Co., p. 78 bottom; Spanish Olive Oil Institute, p. 36 left; Walter Storck, p. 14; Western Growers Association, p. 58, p. 68; Wheat Flour Institute, p. 50, p. 54, p. 64 right, p. 65 left, p. 65 right, p. 86.

Instructions for recipes and safety precautions in this book are in accord with the standards of the U.S. Department of Agriculture and have been carefully checked for accuracy. However, the author and publisher do not warrant or guarantee results and cannot be responsible for any adverse consequences resulting from the use of information contained herein. The author has attempted to assist the reader in avoiding problems by setting forth appropriate and recommended procedures.

Contents

Part I Putting Your Electric Crockery Cooker to Work

1 Slow-Pot Cooking 7
Meal Planning with a Slow Cooker — Timing and Heat
Levels — Slow-Cook Recipes Are Different — The Slow Cooker Cooks
Differently — Savings and the Hospitality Pot — Comfort Foods and
Breakfast

2 How to Use and Care for a Slow Cooker 16
Timing Table — Using a Timer with Your Slow Cooker — Care and
Cleaning of the Crockery Pot — Handle Crockery Cookers with
Care — Don't Uncover the Slow Cooker to Stir — Adjust Recipes to Size
of Your Slow Cooker

Part II Slow-Cooking the Meats

3 Beef and Veal 22
Beef — Veal

4 Pork and Ham 41

5 Chicken, Lamb, and Other Meats 45
Lamb — Other Meats

Part III Soups for Supper — and Luncheon, Too

6 Soups That Begin with Leftovers 56
Saving Other Discards to Make Soup

7 Soups That Make One-Dish Dinners 61

Part IV Vegetables and Side Dishes

8 Casseroles of Vegetable Mélanges 70

9 Side Dishes 75
Beans and Dried Vegetables — Cereals and Grains — The Pastas

Part V Comfort Foods and Desserts

10 Baking and Sweets to Slow Cook 82
Baking in a Slow Cooker — About Baking Recipes — Using the Timer
for Baking — Don't Lift the Lid During Baking — Breakfast
Foods — Puddings, Custards, and Compotes

Index 96

Part I
Putting Your Electric Crockery Cooker to Work

Beef Stew   *This dish is done to perfection in the slow cooker. The recipe appears on page 29.*

6   *Clear & Simple Crockery Cooking*

1
Slow-Pot Cooking

A slow-cook pot, like a blender, brings to its owner a whole new range of cooking possibilities. Learn to fit a blender into your cooking style and it can add dramatically to the variety of foods you serve. Learn to fit a slow cooker into your cooking style, and not only can it improve the variety and flavor of the foods you serve, but it can cut the time you spend in the kitchen almost in half. It can free the working mother and housewife from the kitchen for many hours while the meal is cooking.

A slow cooker doesn't replace the stove top or the oven. It has a particular and well-defined range of possibilities. It cooks foods in a certain way, and the kinds of food done in a slow cooker have a certain similarity. Its specialty is main dishes, casseroles, and soups. It can't produce a roasted effect or a broiled effect (except with last-minute preparation of some dishes). Foods done in slow cookers have the made-from-scratch, slaved-over-a-hot-stove flavor of a good stew. That's not all a slow cooker can do, but it is one of its most important assets.

Meal Planning with a Slow Cooker

In order to figure just where the slow-cook crock pot fits into your meal planning, you have to know what it can do for you and what it can't do for you.

This is easiest, perhaps, to understand if you think of the slow cooker as a large kettle or saucepan that cooks so slowly that no steam escapes from underneath its well-fitted lid. The nearest thing to it is a Dutch oven. A Dutch oven is made of heavy cast iron and has a heavy, heavy lid that keeps most of the steam in. It is usually set over a very low fire and it makes divine stews and casseroles. Most good cooks own one and I've never been in a European household where it wasn't part of the cooking equipment. For generations, American mothers and grandmothers used one at the back of the coal- or wood-burning stove. It is the slowest-cooking piece of equipment we had until the slow-cook electric pot came along a few years ago.

However, there's a difference between a Dutch oven and a slow-cook crockery pot. The Dutch oven caramelizes the sugars (the step before burning is caramelizing, or browning) in the ingredients in it (and that's good), but unwatched it tends to go dry and will burn or dry out the ingredients. You can't go away for hours and leave it to its own devices. You have to check it occasionally to make sure there's enough liquid inside to keep things cooking instead of drying or burning.

The slow-cook pot lets no steam escape. That is the key factor in understanding what it does for, and to, foods. It can take all day to cook almost everything. That's the key factor in understanding how to use it to free yourself from the kitchen without sacrificing the variety of home-cooked foods you can serve.

Timing and Heat Levels

Before we look at the kinds of foods a slow-cook pot can make and how to add these to your repertoire, let's look at timing. Each brand of electric pot has its own way of heating up and its own system for setting heat levels (page 15). However, most brands deal primarily in low and high settings or equivalents that mean the same thing. So most recipes for slow-cook cookery tell you to set the heat to Low or to High.

As a generalization, Low means the foods will be cooking at 200° to 240° F. High means they'll cook at about 300° to 340° F. The recipes in this book most often call for cooking on Low. You can halve the time, or just about cut it in half, by turning the dial on your cooker to High.

The reason most recipes here and in other slow-pot cookbooks suggest low settings for the cooking is that we've all found that we can use the slow-cook pot to give us free time. We can get away from the house for half a day or a whole day and still produce a very good meal by using the slow pot's ability to cook foods for a long time, unsupervised, without ruining them.

The low setting gives you the most free time, whereas the high setting cuts the cooking time or free time in half. On the high setting, the slow-cook pot cooks rather as a Dutch oven does. It can caramelize foods and it can dry them out, just as a Dutch oven does. For the cook who wants to escape from the kitchen, the low setting is the interesting one and the one

whose effects change the style in which you put dishes together — the way you cook, in other words.

Slow-Cook Recipes Are Different

Look at the difference between the way a typical recipe is done on top of the stove or in the oven and the way it is done in a slow-cook pot. It will help you to understand how to use your electric slow-cook pot.

Beef stew is a fairly common item in the repertoire of most cooks. The basic procedure is to heat a Dutch oven or a large skillet and to brown in it onions and chunks of meat. Then you flavor the meat with salt and pepper and your favorite herbs and spices, add water, cover, and cook. As the water dries out, you add more water. You may put vegetables in with the meats (and they'll be slightly overdone when it's all over) or you may hang around the kitchen waiting to add the vegetables at staggered intervals later. The carrots go in first, since they are slow to cook, and potatoes half an hour later, since they cook more quickly than the carrots.

You can cook a beef stew in slow-cook pots in exactly the same way. Brown the meat, turn everything into the slow-cook pot, turn the setting to High, add the vegetables at staggered intervals, and unless you've added a lot of water, check at intervals to make sure the dish isn't drying out.

If you set the slow-cook pot on Low, however, this is the way to make Beef Stew (page 29). Brown the meats as for a conventionally cooked stew. Immediately place the stew vegetables, all of them, in the bottom of the slow cooker, set the meats on top, add to the browning skillet whatever liquid is to go into the dish, scrape up all the caramelized pan juices, turn the liquid into the slow cooker, cover, turn the setting to Low. You can come back to a delicious stew somewhere between 6 to 10 hours later, depending on which brand of electric cooker you have bought.

That's an overview of the difference between cooking in a slow-cook pot and cooking in conventional utensils on top of the stove or in the oven. You need to know more about the slow cooker before you can successfully adapt your own favorite recipes to it, but this gives you a notion of how it all works.

The Slow Cooker Cooks Differently

To get down to some of the details of the difference between conventional cooking and slow-pot cooking:

Slow pots cook vegetables more slowly than they cook meats. That's why you can put the vegetables into the stew at the same time as the meats. Because vegetables cook more slowly, recipes suggest you put them in the pot first and the meats on top.

Slow pots don't allow any moisture to escape. Therefore, recipes for slow-pot cooking cut the amount of liquid required by conventional recipes in half or call for less than half.

Moist ingredients cooked in slow pots yield a lot of their moisture. You have no control over the amount of moisture in any given piece of meat because it varies with the cut and quality. Likewise, the moisture varies from one bean to the next, depending on how long ago it was picked and how much rain fell while it was growing. Therefore, there may be more liquid in the bottom of your slow pot when the cooking is over than you really want. More moisture means a thinner sauce. The way out is painless: You can turn the heat in the slow pot to High, remove the cover, and let the sauce bubble away in steam until it has thickened.

There are loads of other ways to thicken a rather thin sauce produced by the slow pot. The easiest is to make a roux (a mixture of equal parts of melted butter and flour), add the sauce from the slow pot, and simmer until the sauce has thickened. The recipes in the meat section in this book will suggest many other ways of turning the ingredients you've cooked in the slow pot into the kind of rich, delicious casserole Mother used to make.

Not all the things you slow-cook have to be casserole or stewy mixtures. The slow-cook pot was made in heaven to produce the perfect pot

Making a Roux   *Adding flour to butter or margarine, or to fat skimmed from a slow-cooked dish, is the first step in making a roux, a thickener for the rather thin cooking liquids typical of slow-pot dishes. The tricks in making a smooth, thickened sauce are to heat the butter or fat over a very low fire, and to stir quickly as flour indicated by recipe is added.*

Second Step in Thickening Roux   *Next step in thickening slow-crock sauces is to pour the cooking liquid from the slow cooker into the gently simmering roux. Add the hot liquid all at once and stir as quickly as you can. In just seconds, the sauce will smooth and thicken to a creamy consistency. Thin slow-cooker sauces can also be thickened by boiling them rapidly over a medium-hot fire until they have been reduced to the desired consistency.*

roast, and I know of nothing that does more for a good brisket. You can also slow-cook a chicken if you want it ready the minute you come through the door. Though it won't be roast chicken or broiled chicken, it will be good, flavorful chicken as tender as can be. Fish and fresh, moist vegetables are at their best cooked briefly and quickly. I find the slow-cook method isn't of any particular value here, especially for fish, so there are no recipes included for them. (You can steam them on High, but I don't.) But the slow cooker does make great vegetable casseroles and rice dishes, and does wonders for delicious bean dishes we mostly don't have the time or patience to make.

That brings up another area of cooking I've been experimenting with in my slow-cook pots — the use of dried vegetables and cereals and grains. These are delicious and, as nutrition buffs will tell you, often are extremely nutritious. The slow cooker does a wonderful job with these and opens up a whole new area of food flavors — one we haven't dealt with since grandmothers and wood-burning stoves left the kitchen.

Savings and the Hospitality Pot

Here are some other kinds of foods slow-pot cooking adds to your stable of dishes:

Slow-pot cooking is an approximation of the cooking method our grandmothers relied on. In Canada, when my Canadian grandmother was cooking, things were tossed into a big iron kettle and set on the back of a coal-burning stove. In France, when my French grandmother was cooking, they went into a large ceramic pot set on the back of a wood-burning stove. In each case, the foods bubbled ever so slowly all day. Into the pot went almost anything that came to hand. In Sweden, where cold and distances are great, years ago it was a duty to feed anyone who came to the door. Guests scraped their leftovers into a big pot on the stove. New fresh ingredients were added, and so the "hospitality pot" kept going, tasting a little different every day.

The slow pot comes close to being to us what those hospitality kettles were to our grandmothers. It opens the door to cooking possibilities we haven't had available to us for a long time. No one wants the stove-top burner heating all day long. For one thing, it makes the kitchen hot. For another, it costs money. The slow pot's low heat intensity allows it to cook for pennies a day (or for pennies a night, for that matter). And it doesn't heat the kitchen up at all. That means we can think in terms of hospitality pots again.

What this means to me is that I can make stock from saved-up meat bones, cooked and uncooked, and from scraps usually discarded — celery leaves, carrot trimmings, onion leaves that didn't allow me to mince them and normally get thrown away. Meat stock, or bouillon, is the secret of superior cooking when it comes to gravies, stews, casseroles, and braising meats and vegetables. In the past, I used water plus Steero granules or other brand bouillon cubes to make hasty bouillon, broth, or stock to cook with. With the coming of slow-pot cooking to my house, I use discards and leftovers to make bouillon or stock. Instead of just adding flavor to my dishes, I'm adding nutrition, and it costs next to nothing.

The stock pot becomes a soup pot when you add not only discards but the ingredients for dinner. Soup from a can may be okay for luncheon sandwiches if there's nothing else available, but soup that includes a chicken or a piece of beef or a delicious combination of vegetables or beans makes a wonderful and different dinner. Who said we have to have meat and potatoes every night? Try one of the hearty soups in Chapter 7, "Soups That Make One-Dish Dinners." In less than half an hour you can make wonderful hot biscuits (use a mix — they're great) to go with the soup. Offer lots of butter with the biscuits, add a salad and a nice dessert, and even the most meat-and-potatoes person in the household will tell you it's a treat. A soup dinner will feed multitudes for very little. It's romantic: That's what our grandmothers served very often for family suppers. Making soup in a slow cooker only needs minutes of your time in the morning, leaving you free for the rest of the day.

Beans of Every Kind   *The slow cooker makes the most of protein-rich dried legumes of all sorts, from red beans to navy beans.*

Comfort Foods and Breakfast

One more historic item the slow-cook pot makes possible is an old-fashioned breakfast. Whether or not you like to eat in the morning, we're told the morning meal is the most important. In our hurry-up lives, the notion of rising at six to spend an hour cooking breakfast is not appealing to the majority. So — let the slow-cook pot bring breakfast back into your life.

The slow cooker cooks overnight as happily and inexpensively as it cooks during the day. The wonderfully nutty cereals, dripping with butter or swimming in cream (or milk if you prefer), are real body builders for children and make a good sound basis for starting a demanding day. Made from whole grains that have simmered all night in the slow pot, they are a totally different affair from the textureless, washed-out flavor of the quick-cook cereals. Even those who don't much like eating in the morning find them worthwhile.

You can make more thrilling breakfast foods than cereals with the slow-cook pot. If you add an electric timer (which works like the appliances that turn on the lights when you are away to keep burglars at bay), you can have cornmeal cakes and blueberry muffins ready when you get up. Or fresh, hot, orange or banana nut bread. Or wonderfully sweet sticky buns no child and few adults can resist.

Or if you want to get into some serious eating in the morning, the slow cooker opens the horizon to things like steak and kidney pie. It takes a little extra time to prepare, but nothing like the time it takes without a slow cooker to assist.

2
How to Use and Care for a Slow Cooker

There are more than two dozen brands of electric slow cookers on the market now and more turning up all the time. As the popularity of the slow pot grows, industry copies the most successful models and produces yet other versions.

I'm assuming that, since you are reading this book, you have or wish to buy a slow cooker. In understanding the recipes adapted for slow cookers and in understanding the slow cooker itself, the most important and the only mysterious element is timing.

Slow-cook recipes give a much wider leeway in cooking times than do other recipes, depending on which cooker you buy. A span of 2 hours is common. "Turn to Low and cook, covered, 6 to 8 hours" is a common instruction. When you are cooking on High, the recipe instruction halves the time — "3 to 4 hours."

That span of hours — 2 on Low or 1 on High — means this: On Low, the recipe may be expected to be done at the earliest in 6 hours in some electric cookers and at the latest in 8 hours in others. On High, it may be done at the earliest in 3 hours or at the latest in 4 hours.

If you've just acquired a slow cooker, how do you know whether dinner will be ready at six o'clock or at eight o'clock?

Adjust recipe timing to your slow cooker. Learning the timing pattern of your cooker is the first — almost the only — thing you have to do to be successful with slow-cook recipes. The timing instructions in this book are a little shorter than the slowest of the slow pots on the market. The Timing Table in this chapter suggests cooking patterns for the slow pots I've studied, but they are only *indications*. I have found that slow cookers with instructions to cook at exactly the same heating curve don't. They vary and you will soon learn how slow your pot cooks. I cut a pork rib roast in half and put each half in a different slow pot. I was informed that both pots cooked exactly the same way — and found that the roast in one cooked long before the other. I've tested two different slow-cooker models made by the same manufacturer and found they cooked at slightly different speeds. Disclaimers in slow-cooker literature warn that line surges and other peculiarities of electrical current affect the cooking times.

What all these variables mean is the slow cooker in your kitchen has its own

For Garnish   *In foreground, finely minced onion; in background, coarsely chopped onion.*

For Garnish   *In foreground, finely minced parsley; in background, chopped parsley.*

heating pattern. The timing of recipes are indications but not absolutes. Expect for the first week or two of slow cooking to find things done a little earlier or later than predicted. Check the slow-cooker contents an hour earlier — or two hours earlier in very long-cooking recipes — until you get the hang of the cooking pattern of your own particular model.

Even if the foods are ready earlier than predicted, they won't be harmed. They may be a little overdone, but they won't be dried out or burned because the slow cooker lets no steam escape — remember Chapter 1 — and slow cookers cook so gently and so slowly that foods aren't likely to be very much overdone. Dense cuts of beef (pot roast in the round, for instance) are stringy and dry when overdone. But the slow cooker makes a delicious sauce as it cooks the meat, so you can ladle lots of this over the meat slices if they've dried out a little.

Once you understand your cooker's particular timing, you will know how to adjust your recipe timing instructions so things come up perfect.

Many, perhaps most, slow-cook recipes are almost impossible to overdo, by the way. Casseroles and stews and vegetable mélanges are delicious only when they cook slowly for hours. You really do have the two, four, or more hours the majority of recipes give you.

At the end of that time, you immediately add the quickly cooked ingredients, fast prepared seasonings, or garnishes that finish off superb dishes as though you had just spent two hours or more in the kitchen.

Chopped parsley, chives, or onions are among the most essential last-minute touches for the freshest looking dishes that have really cooked, to delicious completion, for hours.

Timing Table

Recipes in this book have been timed to slow pots that cook at somewhere between 200° F. to 240° F. on Low and 300° F. to 340° F. on High. Study the cooking heats described for your model. Check the table opposite, which describes cooking curves for the several brands of slow cookers. Then try one of the recipes in this book, using your adjustment on timing. The results will tell you whether you need to shorten cooking times or lengthen them.

Timing Table and Chart of Heat Levels

Brand name of electric slow cooker Note: These are *not* pressure cookers	For Low Cook at	For High Cook at
CORNING ELECTROMATIC TABLE RANGE 2½ qts. Note: Halve recipes in this book for this unit, and add half a cup of liquid, as it dries foods more than do the other types of cookers. When baking, add half a cup of water to the unit and use a trivet. It really isn't designed for slow baking.	240° F	350° F
CORNWALL CROCKERY COOKER 4 qts.	Med.	Hi
CORNWALL TRAY MODEL CROCKERY COOKER 2½ qts. Note: Halve recipes. Add at least half a cup of water to recipes that do not call for a liquid when using this as a slow cooker. Use ½ cup more liquid in recipes that do call for liquids. The first few times you use the unit for slow cooking, make notes on how much difference there was between actual cooking times and cooking times in the recipes, and how much extra liquid was needed. When baking, add half a cup of water to the pot bottom, and use a trivet.	No. 3 Heat	Do not use
CORNWALL TRAY MODEL COOKER 4½ qts. Note: Add a cup of water to this cooker when recipes call for no water; use ½ cup more liquid to recipes including liquids. When baking, add half a cup of water to the pot bottom and use a trivet. Watch the pot the first few times you use it for slow cooking or for slow baking, to see if timing for recipes here fits, and to test how much extra liquid is needed.	No. 2	No. 3
CORNWALL TRAY MODEL CROCKERY COOKER 8 qts. Note: See notes for 4½-quart Cornwall on adding water. If you double recipes to fill the 8-quart container, use regular cooking times; if you use recipes as written, reduce cooking time by an hour or two. This cooker tends to cook fast.	No. 2 Heat	No. 3 Heat
DOMINION CROCK-A-DIAL 3 qts. Note: This model seems to cook a little more slowly than most.	Low	High
EMPIRE EASY MEAL SLOW COOKER 2½ qts. Note: Halve recipes, and add a little extra liquid, about half a cup. Watch the pot the first few times you use this unit with the recipes here, to gauge how closely its cooking time fits the recipes, and how much extra liquid may be needed.	Medium	Between Medium and High
FARBERWARE POT-POURRI 3 and 5 qts. Note: These units cook more quickly than the recipes here indicate. Reduce cooking times for recipes by about ⅓, and watch the pot the first few times to gauge timing.	200° F	300° F

	For Low Cook at	For High Cook at
GRANDINETTI CROCKERY COOK POT 3½ and 5 qts.	Low	High
Note: For 3½ quart unit, keep recipe ingredients on the skimpy side. A few recipes may not quite fit the pot size.		
HAMILTON BEACH CONTINENTAL COOKER	Low	High
CROCK-WATCHER	Low	High
SIMMER-ON	Low	High
Note: The Continental Cooker and the Crock-Watcher have auto-shift controls that start foods on a hotter setting than the real Low. In combination with the auto-shift hot-cook period, the Low setting ends up cooking foods at about the same pace as the recipes here indicate. Without the auto-shift, on Low, these cookers cook more slowly than recipes indicate. Study your model the first few times you use it, and adjust recipes according to its performance.		
NESCO POT LUCK COOKER 4½ qts.	200° F	250° F
Notes: Steam escapes through holes in the lid, and this means you lose some of the liquid in the recipe. Add another quarter or half cup of liquid to recipes, or block the holes in the lid with crumpled pieces of foil. This model cooks a little faster than recipes here indicate. Watch your pot the first few times you use recipes from this book, and adjust cooking periods to the pattern of your pot, if necessary		
OSTER SUPER POT 8 qts.	200° F	300° F
Note: This unit cooks faster than the times given here. Reduce the time planned for slow-cook recipes by about 2 hours, and fast-cook recipes (on High in this book) by about half. If you double the ingredients in recipes to fill the capacity of this big unit, cooking times as stated in the book may be about right. The first few times you use the unit, keep an eye on the contents to gauge how closely it comes to cooking at the speeds indicated in the book.		
PENNEY'S SLOW COOKER/FRYER 4 qts.	Just left of the crockery cooking band	Between 325° and 350° F
PRESTO SLOW COOKERS 2¾ and 5 qts.	High	Between High and Brown
Note: Halve ingredients in recipes for the 2¾-quart model. Reduce cooking times by about 2 hours on slow-cook recipes in this book when you are using this unit, and reduce time for High-cook recipes by about half. Study the time your unit takes to cook, compare timing with timing given for the recipes here, particularly for baking. The smaller unit really isn't suited to baking.		

	For Low Cook at	For High Cook at
REGAL MARDI GRAS POT O' PLENTY 4 qts. Note: This unit cooks a little faster than recipes here, and the pot may need stirring. Study the way your model handles meats, and adjust your cooking plans accordingly. It pays to add a little more water to the recipes until you have a notion of how your model performs.	No. 2 Heat	No. 3 Heat
RIVAL CROCK POTS 3, 4½, and 5 qts.	Low	High
SEARS CROCKERY COOKER 4½ qts.	Med	Hi
SEARS TRAY MODEL 2½ qts. Note: Halve recipes. This unit doesn't seem to cook fast enough to use High treatment given for recipes in this book. Add a cup of water to this cooker when recipes call for no liquid, and add half a cup more liquid to recipes including liquids. When baking, add half a cup of water to the pot bottom, and use a trivet. Not really suited to slow baking.	No. 3 Heat	Do not use High recipes
SEARS TRAY MODEL 5 qts. Note: Add a cup of water to this cooker when recipes call for no liquid, and add half a cup more liquid to recipes including liquids. When baking, add half a cup of water to the pot bottom, and use a trivet.	No. 2 Heat	No. 3 Heat
SUNBEAM CROCKER COOKER 4½ qts. Note: Recipes come out just right if you set the dial just left of the crockery cooker band.	Just left of crockery cooker band	between 325° F and 350° F
SUNBEAM CROCKER FRYPAN 2 qts. Note: Halve the recipes in this book, and add ½ to 1 cup of liquid per recipe, including to recipes where no liquid is called for. Watch the pot the first few times you use it for recipes here, to gauge the differences between its way of cooking and those indicated in the recipes.	200° F	300° F
WARDS AND VAN WYCK SIM-R-WARE 4 qts. Note: The High setting may cook a little faster than the recipes given here.	High	Do not use High recipes
WEST BEND LAZY DAY SLO-COOKER 5 qts.	No. 2 Heat	No. 4 Heat

The timings for most slow-pot recipes are pretty standard, and they reflect the cooking curves of the slower units, not the faster ones.

Don't let all this information on timing make you feel it is a problem to get the timing for your slow-pot cooker just right. To get dishes cooked properly with a stove, you must know the stove. The same thing applies to the slow cooker.

Using a Timer with Your Slow Cooker

A timer gives you complete control over the length of time you want to leave your crock pot to do the cooking. A timer — an electrical fixture that goes into the wall socket and turns the slow cooker on and off at specific periods — costs from under $10 to about $25. I've recommended its use especially in Part V, "Comfort Foods and Desserts." You can wake up to the aroma of fresh-baked orange nut bread for breakfast by using a timer. Slow cookers can bake while you sleep, but they generally bake on a high setting and for fewer hours than most of us spend in bed. By placing

the ingredients in the slow cooker and setting a timer to turn the slow cooker on so that the food will be ready for breakfast, you get around that problem.

You can use a timer to start all the other foods you cook in a slow pot. If a dish calls for 5 to 7 cooking hours and you want to be away 10 hours, the timer will make that possible. In my view a timer is a really good investment for the slow-pot cook.

The question of whether there will be spoilage in foods that sit around in the slow pot waiting to be turned on by a timer does come up. I wouldn't choose a boiling hot day and an easily spoiled meat like chicken for timed cooking. If you are concerned about using the timer for a casserole that has ingredients susceptible to spoilage, keep all the casserole ingredients in the refrigerator until you are ready to combine the dish and use ice cubes, added just before you leave the house, as the liquid content. The cubes will melt slowly, keeping everything cool until the cooking starts.

Electric Timing *An electric timer can be used with a slow-cook pot. With the cooker turned on to the proper setting and the timer plugged into the electric wall switch, food will start heating at hour for which timer is set, whether you are home or not. You can set the crock pot in the morning when you leave the house, have a dish cook six or eight hours and be ready when you arrive home in the evening. If set for the proper length of cooking time, the heat will go off even if you are late arriving home.*

Care and Cleaning of the Crockery Pot

There are three major types of crockery pots. The pot can be a tray model container that sits on a heating unit like a small single burner. There are pots whose crockery is part of the heating unit and also pots that go into, or are part of, a larger container that has heating wires around its walls. If you have a choice, I think you will find that the last two — the pot within a pot and the crockery cookers that are part of the heating unit — are the easiest to work with. However, the units that sit on heating elements work perfectly well as long as the temperature settings correspond to those intended for the recipes you are using.

Tray models, when made of crockery (some are enamel-coated metal), may crack if no liquid is included in the recipes: Include ¼ cup or more of bouillon, wine, or water if you find it drying out. Liquid is added precisely because steam is escaping and the interior of the crock is getting dry. You needn't worry that the extra liquid will change the recipe; it should evaporate.

Pot with Heating Unit *Slow-cook pot whose crockery container is part of the heating unit is one of the most popular models. It heats evenly and slowly. This model, 4½ quarts, is large enough to hold Pyrex baking cups, a 3-quart casserole, or large soufflé dish for baking cakes and fruit breads and custards or compotes.*

Separate Heating Unit *Slow-cook pot whose crockery container is a separate unit. The heating container, left, can also be used for deep frying. Both types of cookers are more successful than the tray models when slow cooking is your object.*

Crockery cookers that are one piece — that is, cookers in which the cooking unit contains the wiring that heats it — generally should not be immersed in water for washing. That makes keeping the pot clean a little more awkward than when you are working with units whose cooking pot can be removed from the container holding the heating wires. But still it's not much more trouble than an electric coffee pot, and we've all become used to washing those without soaking the electrical cord contact.

If the baked-on food inside the pot is especially greasy, try soaking a few tablespoons of ammonia in the pot. Wash the unit thoroughly after the ammonia has been poured out.

If a lot of food has been baked onto the inside

of a wired unit, fill it with hot soapy water and a few tablespoons of baking soda and set it by the sink for a few hours. If the baked-on food doesn't rinse off easily, scrub it out with a plastic scouring pad. Interiors that are enamel or metal stay new longer if steel wool and cleaning compounds are avoided. It is important that you not scrape or scratch the inside surface of crockery pots. The baked-on glaze can be damaged, and the result will be that foods will stick to the scratched places in the future. If your crockery unit stains, simmer 3 or 4 tablespoons of Teflon cleaner in the pot for an hour; that should cleanse it.

Units coated with Teflon, as are some of the tray models, should be washed thoroughly before first use, then coated lightly with oil to season the interior for the first cooking session. Avoid the use of sharp knives and utensils that can scratch or damage the interior. Wash the Teflon only with plastic cleaners. Teflon in some shades discolors after a time, but the change of color doesn't change its nonstick qualities. Manufacturers' products for cleaning stained Teflon are available. After a stain-removal session, scrub away the cleaning product, wash the interior of the pot thoroughly, and coat again with oil to season before the next cooking session.

Handle Crockery Cookers with Care

Each slow cooker has instructions for its care and handling. Follow them.

Be wary of extreme or sudden changes of temperature with cooking units made of crockery. If yours is a removable unit, don't be tempted to store it in the refrigerator with leftovers and then place it directly from the refrigerator into or onto the heating unit. Sudden application of heat to ice-cold crockery can break it. I never heat my crockery on the stove top. Crockery was once used for stove-top cooking, but eventually the crockery always broke. That's one reason it was replaced by metal saucepans and pots. Think of crockery the way you think of glass. Handled gently, it will last practically forever.

(Glass pots such as those made by Corning are able to stand up to quick changes in temperature; if yours is one of these units, you may use it for freezer or refrigerator storage if you wish.)

Don't Uncover the Slow Cooker to Stir

All slow-cook recipes should be cooked covered until the moment they are ready. You may have to uncover the unit to decide whether it is completely done, but don't uncover it until it is time to test it. The heat inside the units builds up slowly, and every time you uncover the unit, you lose enough heat to slow the cooking process even more. Because the food inside retains all the moisture originally there, ingredients cooking on Low will not dry out or burn. So — there's no need to peek and no need to stir.

Adjust Recipes to Size of Your Slow Cooker

The recipes in this cookbook were worked out with units about 4½ quarts in size. Three-, 3½-, 4-, and 5-quart slow cookers will handle most recipes here. For smaller units, cut the ingredients in half. For the slow cooker to cook at about the recommended times, it should be about half full.

Part II
Slow-Cooking the Meats

3
Beef and Veal

Turning lesser cuts of meat into delicious stews and casseroles is the special talent of the slow cooker. It bubbles ingredients together ever so slowly for hours and hours, and the end product has a flavor you don't get any other way.

Among the recipes in this book are many you will recognize as classic, from Coq au Vin to Boeuf Bourgignon and Irish Stew. I've adapted family recipes to cooking in a slow pot. I start stews and casseroles as for conventional cooking by browning the meats in a skillet. You can omit this step if you want to and with it the oil or fat the meats are to be browned in. However, if you do omit it, you will not have the rich flavor of skillet-browned meat juices in your stew, and the flavor will be much more bland. Browning the meats, then scraping up the juices in the pan with the liquid that is to go into the stew, is the real secret of a stew or casserole with a rich flavor.

Because the slow cooker tends to cook vegetables more slowly than meats, you will notice that almost all recipes call for placing vegetables under the meats in the slow cooker. In using the recipes here as guides for adapting your own favorite recipes to the slow cooker, remember to place the vegetables under — not on top. Meat loaf is an exception to this. The tomatoes that garnish the top of the loaf are canned, that is, already cooked, and they look better on top.

Almost all the recipes in this section include some liquid in the ingredients. A few include only vegetables. These will yield their moisture, as will the meats, and make a sauce for the dish. However, a few include no liquid in the ingredients list and no vegetables. There are some slow cookers on the market which require that some liquid be present before the dish begins to cook. If yours is such a model, when you come to a recipe that doesn't call for the addition of a liquid, just add whatever minimum amount of liquid your particular brand requires. Use meat stock, or beef bouillon granules or cubes, rather than plain water. Or you may use tomato juice if that seems appropriate.

Let me repeat Chapter 2's caution about cooking times. Each make of slow cooker has its own way of heating up and its own heat levels. They are all somewhat different, in my experience, including those meant to cook exactly the same way. Furthermore, I have found differences in cooking times between

Caramelizing *Scrape up pan juices with a spatula. Meats caramelize when browned in a skillet before they are put into the slow-pot, creating the "meaty" flavor we associate with roast, stews and hearty casseroles. Since the slow cooker doesn't produce the "caramelized" flavor, many recipes in this book recommend browning meats before they are put into the cooker. It isn't necessary — but it adds considerably to the savor of the dish, particularly to that of meat stews.*

models by the same maker. Get to know the cooking timing of your own particular slow cooker and let that information guide you when planning cooking times for the recipes in this and your other slow-cooker recipe books.

One other thing that will be helpful in pacing cooking times: A big chunk of solid meat that is ice cold from the refrigerator will take longer to cook in the slow cooker than one that has been warmed to room temperature. Temperatures in the slow cooker are low; ice-cold meat inside the cooker makes it that much slower to get up to its cooking heat. In one or two recipes I've specified meat at room temperature. The others are timed for meats just from the refrigerator. If your slow cooker seems to cook even more slowly than my recipe timings indicate and you want to cut, rather than lengthen, the cooking times, always allow meat to warm to room temperature before placing it in the cooker.

Beef

Most beef slow-cook recipes give you 8 to 10 or more hours of free time. A slow-cook crockery pot is the answer to the problem of what to do — that will taste great — with the less expensive and rather tougher cuts of beef.

There are lots of basic beef cuts, and these fall into two categories. There is beef with lots of gristle and fat running through the meat, and there is beef that is a solid chunk of rather dense meat. Tender steaks — sirloin, for instance, and roasts such as prime ribs — are marbled with veins of fat. These are the expensive cuts and they are best cooked at high temperatures. Under extremes of heat, the fat in these cuts melts while the meat tissue around is cooking rapidly, and the end result is a well-browned, tender roast or steak.

The less tender cuts of beef respond badly to high heats. Gristle tenderizes so slowly during the cooking process that if you cook meats that have a lot of gristle quickly, the meaty parts will have cooked almost to a shoe-leather state before the gristle has broken down. With the exception of filet mignon (the most tender cut of the whole animal), beef that is a chunk of solid meat tends to be rather tough; cooked quickly, it often gets tougher yet and can require more chewing than gum.

However, when they are cooked very, very slowly, the lesser cuts of meat become tender. These days, most of us start the average family meal not by looking for a recipe but rather by looking at the meat counter to see what's on special. When you have a slow cooker in the kitchen, think in these terms: Gristly, fatty cuts such as brisket (not inexpensive anymore, alas) and chuck are excellent done in the slow cooker whole, pot-roast style, while dense, lean meats that are rather tough (as, for instance, top round and sirloin tip) are best cut up and stewed in the cooker casserole style with vegetables and sauces. Bottom round and better grades of aged top round can also be cooked in the slow cooker. But why not roast these?

If you try to do every meal in a slow cooker, there'll be a sameness to the menu that is tiresome. The more variety meals offer, the more each dish is appreciated.

Many of your favorite recipes for hamburger and ground round can be done in a slow cooker. However, ground beef is excellent when cooked quickly at fairly high heats and doesn't really need the slow-cook process to be especially good. Therefore, I haven't included many ground-beef recipes. You will find recipes for meat sauce, meatballs, and meat loaf at the end of the beef section. Use these basic methods to adapt your own favorite ground-beef recipes to slow cooking.

Meats with bones in them — large bones — present a problem for the slow cooker. Not all bone-in cuts fit into every cooker. Slow cookers come in many shapes and sizes, but none as large as an oven that will take any size bone-in piece. When buying large, bone-in meat to be done as a whole piece in your cooker, remember that it has to fit the cooker both in size and in shape. Stew pieces of beef that include bones are among the tastiest, and these, of course, fit into any cooker since the pieces are small.

The beef cuts I've used in the recipes that follow are found most everywhere. Other similar cuts can be used instead. In every recipe, I've suggested the cut that seems to be best for the recipe. However, you can substitute top round for bottom round, and sirloin tip for top round. If you use stew meat that is already cut up and find that the recipe calls for 2-inch pieces, while your meat is in 1½-inch pieces or in 2½-inch pieces, you may need to adjust the cooking time by an hour or so. The smaller pieces of meat can take a little less time, the larger pieces a little more time.

Here are the cuts I've found the slow cooker does wonders for:

Chuck steak and roasts, boneless or bone-in
Chuck stew beef
Bottom round
Top round
Rump steak
Brisket
Beef shank cross-cut
Pot roast, chuck or rump
Round steak
Flank steak
Short ribs of beef

There are others, and in your area these cuts may have another name. The principles described above will help you sort one from the other and make the right choices. The basic rule is: If it's tough or gristly, the slow cooker will do a lot for it, but you can cook any meat in the slow pot if you want a slow-cook approach to getting dinner, one that leaves you free for half the day, or a whole day.

Slow-Cooked Barbecue
3 to 5 hours

This is a good recipe to use for a pick-up meal after a party. Serve on toasted hamburger rolls with a mixed garden salad.

1½ lb. boneless chuck steak, 1½ inches thick	1 tsp. paprika
	2 Tbs. Worcestershire sauce
1 clove garlic, peeled and minced	½ cup ketchup
	1 tsp. salt
¼ cup wine vinegar	1 tsp. dry or prepared mustard
1 Tbs. brown sugar	¼ tsp. black pepper

To Cook: Cut the beef on a diagonal, across the grain, into slices 1 inch wide. Place these in a slow cooker. In a small bowl, combine the remaining ingredients and pour over the meat. Mix the meat and the sauce. Cover and cook on Low for 3 to 5 hours.
Makes 4 to 5 servings.

Walter Fischman's Red Beef Appetizer
8 to 10 hours

This is a Chinese way with beef, well suited to dense, rather tough cuts such as top round. Cooled and sliced thinly, Red Beef makes a great appetizer, especially for an Oriental meal.

½ cup soy sauce	2 to 3 slices fresh or frozen ginger, minced
¼ cup dry sherry	
2 cups water	
2 heaping tsp. light brown sugar	1½ lb. top round of beef
3 scallions, minced	

To Cook: Place all the ingredients in the slow cooker, cover, and cook on Low, 8 to 10 hours, or until tender.

Before Serving: Allow the beef to cool in the cooking liquid, then drain, slice thinly across the grain, and serve.
Makes 10 to 12 servings.

Paupiettes de Boeuf
5 to 7 hours

This dish takes time to prepare before it is ready for the slow cooker. It's a really delicious and distinctly different French gourmet recipe, nice with Beaujolais wine.

2 Tbs. butter	1 lb. bottom round of
2 medium onions,	beef, cut into 16
peeled and finely	thin slices, each 4
minced	inches square
½ lb. fresh mush-	Salt
rooms, wiped	Pepper
clean and minced	Ground thyme
1 Tbs. grated lemon	All-purpose flour
rind	4 Tbs. butter
2 Tbs. unflavored	1 cup warm water
bread crumbs	2 medium cloves
½ cup fresh, minced	garlic, peeled and
parsley	crushed
1 tsp. salt	2 Tbs. prepared
¼ tsp. pepper	mustard, pref-
2 eggs, slightly	erably Maille or
beaten	white Dijon

To Cook: In a heavy skillet, over medium-low heat, melt the 2 tablespoons of butter and sauté the onions and the mushrooms until the onions are translucent. Stir in the lemon rind, bread crumbs, parsley, salt, and pepper. When the parsley has wilted — about 1 minute after you add it to the skillet — quickly stir in the beaten eggs to bind the mixture and remove the skillet from the heat at once. Set aside. With a rolling pin or a wooden mallet, flatten the beef pieces until each is very thin and about twice its original size. As you finish each piece, season it with a little salt, pepper, and a pinch of thyme. At the widest end of each beef slice, place a teaspoon of bread-crumb mixture from the skillet and roll up the meat, sausage-shape, and secure it with a wooden toothpick through the center. Roll each piece in flour. In a very large skillet, over medium-high heat, melt the 4 tablespoons of butter, and brown the pieces of beef. As you finish, place them in the slow cooker. Pour the water into the skillet, scrape up the pan juices and add. Turn the sauce into the cooker, cover, and cook on Low for about 5 hours.

Before Serving: About half an hour before serving, mix the garlic and the mustard into the sauce around the beef, cover, turn the heat to High, and cook for 30 minutes. If the sauce seems less flavorful than you like, about 5 minutes before serving add another dab of prepared mustard and a little more salt. If the sauce seems thin, leave the cover off during this second cooking period.
Makes 6 to 8 servings.

Flank Steak with Sablaise Stuffing
8 to 10 hours

The difference between this recipe and the Flank Steak Pot Roast (next page) is in the stuffing. Follow all the directions for the Flank Steak Pot Roast, but substitute the following stuffing:

3 Tbs. butter or	½ cup minced parsley
margarine	1 whole egg, slightly
½ lb. mushrooms,	beaten
minced fine	1 tsp. grated lemon
1 large clove garlic,	rind
peeled and minced	Salt
1 cup minced onion	Pepper
	Ground thyme

In a large skillet, over medium heat, melt the butter or margarine, and sauté the mushrooms for about 2 minutes. Add the garlic and the onions, and sauté for another minute or two, until the onion becomes translucent. Add the parsley and sauté, stirring constantly, about 1 minute, or until the parsley turns dark green. Immediately stir in the whole egg; it acts as a binder only and shouldn't cook more than a minute, just enough so that the white of the egg is congealed and stops being transparent. Remove the skillet at once from the stove and add salt, pepper, and ground thyme to suit your taste.

Beef à l'Estouffade
10 to 12 hours

This is a dish associated with the romance of French peasant life. It is served at family dinners right from the cooking pot and accompanied by big chunks of crusty French bread. Since it cooks for a very long time, it's a great way to prepare lesser cuts of meat. The original recipe calls for canned truffles. Since truffles are hard to come by and worth their weight in gold, I use a mixture of mushroom stems and grated lemon rind to approximate the flavoring the truffle gives to the dish.

½ cup minced fresh mushroom stems	4 oz. pitted green olives
½ tsp. grated lemon rind	1 large bay leaf
1 large clove garlic, peeled and sliced	¼ tsp. ground thyme
	4 whole cloves
2 pork hocks	4 whole peppercorns
6 small carrots, scraped and sliced	2 tsp. salt
½ lb. mushrooms, wiped and stemmed	1 large sprig fresh parsley or ½ tsp. dried parsley
1 green pepper, seeded, peeled, and thinly sliced	4 lb. top round of beef, cut in a square piece
	2 cups dry red wine

To Cook: In a small bowl, preferably one with a rough surface, such as wood, mash the mushroom caps, green pepper, olives, bay leaf, make a paste. Place the pork hocks, carrots, mushroom caps, green pepper, olives, bay leaf, thyme, cloves, peppercorns, salt, and parsley in the slow cooker. Set the beef on top, and cover the beef with the mushroom and lemon-rind paste. Pour the wine into the cooker, cover, and cook on Low for 10 to 12 hours.

Before Serving: After cooking, the sauce will be rather thin. If you would like it a little thicker, pour it into a small skillet and simmer until thickened.

Makes 10 to 12 servings.

Flank Steak Pot Roast
8 to 10 hours

The preparations for this are a little like making a jelly roll and take me about 35 minutes. You'll need skewers or wooden toothpicks to hold the meat in a roll.

1 flank steak (about 2 lb.)	1 tsp. wine vinegar
	½ cup hot water
1 cup unflavored bread crumbs	½ tsp. whole peppercorns
¼ cup minced onion	2 Tbs. butter or margarine
1 Tbs. minced parsley	
½ tsp. salt	¼ cup all-purpose flour
¼ tsp. black pepper	
½ tsp. ground sage	1 Tbs. soy sauce or Worcestershire sauce
1 Tbs. butter or margarine	
1 Tbs. vegetable oil	½ cup bouillon

To Cook: On a slant, contrary to the grain of the meat, slash one side of the steak. Turn the steak slashed side down. In a medium bowl, combine crumbs, onion, parsley, salt, pepper, and sage. Cover the steak with this stuffing, leaving half an inch free all around the edges. Smooth the stuffing firmly into place and dot with the 1 tablespoon of butter or margarine. Roll up the steak, like a jelly roll, starting at the side opposite the widest edge. If a little stuffing spills, tuck it back into the ends after the steak has been rolled up. Secure with skewers or wooden toothpicks. In a medium skillet, over medium-high heat, brown the meat on all sides in the vegetable oil, then lift it into the slow cooker and dribble the vinegar over the top. To the hot oil in the skillet, add the water; scrape up the pan juices and pour them over the meat. Sprinkle with peppercorns. Cover, and cook on Low for 8 to 10 hours.

Before Serving: In a medium skillet, over medium-low heat, melt the 2 tablespoons of butter or margarine and stir in the flour. Pour the juices from the cooker and soy or Worcestershire sauce into the mixture and stir quickly to a smooth sauce. If the sauce seems too thick, add a little hot bouillon or water; usually there's a lot of juice left in the bottom of the cooker when you remove the meat, so add that to thin the sauce. If the sauce seems too thin, simmer a few minutes to reduce and thicken it. Serve with the meat.

Makes 4 to 5 servings.

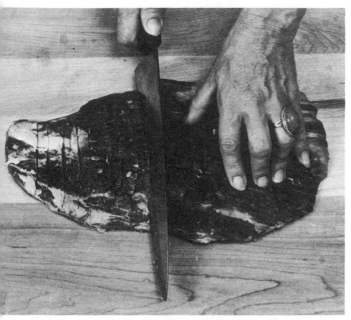

Slashing the flank steak contrary to the grain of the meat, which runs in the direction of the long lines of fat.

Don't slash all the way through. Turn slashed side down, and place stuffing on the uncut side.

Steak is rolled up lengthwise around the stuffing, like a jelly roll. Stretch the meat to fit, and don't compact the stuffing too much or it won't be as good.

Skewering the edges of the steak with toothpicks. Tuck any spilled stuffing neatly into the open ends of the roll before skewering them.

Walter Fischman's Thinning Pot Roast
8 to 10 hours

This is a pot roast Walter makes from the cut sold in New York as a California pot roast: it's chuck beef. Thickened with dried mixed vegetables, which you'll find in foreign food markets at reasonable prices, the sauce tastes like the richest, most delicious of gravies, but is relatively calorie-free.

3 lb. chuck pot roast	2 large cloves garlic, peeled and minced
1½ cups beef bouillon (College Inn) or 1½ cups water with Steero beef granules	½ tsp. dried thyme
	1 Tbs. chili powder
	2 tsp. dried lemon peel
½ cup dry red wine	2 Tbs. soy sauce
2 tsp. salt	1 cup mixed dried vegetables
½ tsp. pepper	

To Cook: Place all the ingredients in the slow cooker, cover, and cook on Low for 8 to 10 hours.

Before Serving: Remove the beef to a serving dish and keep warm. Put the cooking liquids and everything into a blender and blend them until liquefied. (If there's too much for the blender, turn the stock into a saucepan and simmer to reduce, then blend.) Remove and discard fat as it rises to the top of the blender. Pour the thick, rich sauce over the meat and serve.
Makes 8 to 10 servings.

Pot au Feu
12 to 18 hours

This is boiled beef, one of the favorites of all French family dishes. It is perfect only when it is slow cooked. At home, we serve it in a soup bowl with big chunks of crusty French bread. You may select a rump pot roast for this; other choices are bottom round, sirloin tip, or chuck pot roast. Leftover veal scraps and a marrow bone or two can be added.

3 lb. rump pot roast	1 can (10 oz.) beef bouillon or 10 oz. water and 2 beef bouillon cubes
4 chicken wings or equivalent in chicken necks, backs, and gizzards	
	1 small onion, peeled and stuck with 4 whole cloves
3 large carrots, scraped and quartered	1 large bay leaf
	6 sprigs fresh parsley or 1 tsp. dried parsley
3 parsnips or 3 medium young white turnips, scraped	½ tsp. ground thyme
	4 cloves garlic, peeled (optional)
3 large stalks celery, cut into 4-inch pieces	8 peppercorns
	2 to 3 tsp. salt

Sea salt or coarse kosher salt, if available

To Cook: Place all the ingredients, except the sea salt, in the slow cooker, with the vegetables and herbs on the bottom. Cover and cook on Low for 12 to 18 hours. Discard chicken pieces. Serve from a tureen into soup dishes. Offer the sea salt on the side. It is meant to be sprinkled over the meat by each diner before eating.
Makes 5 to 6 servings.

Simple Beef Curry
6 to 8 hours

This is an easy curry sauce made with bottom round and meant to be served with plain boiled rice, though it's nice with noodles, too.

1 large onion, peeled, chopped	1 Tbs. curry powder
1 large clove garlic, peeled, minced	2 cups beef bouillon or 2 cups water with Steero beef bouillon granules
3 Tbs. butter or oil	
1 lb. bottom round of beef, cut in 1-inch cubes	

To Cook: In a large skillet, over medium-high heat, sauté the onion and the garlic in the butter until the onion is beginning to turn dark gold. Add the meat cubes and the curry powder and sauté until browned on all sides. Turn the meat into the slow cooker. Add the beef bouillon to the skillet and scrape up the pan juices. Turn into the slow cooker, cover, and cook on Low for 6 to 8 hours, or until the meat is tender.

Before Serving: If the sauce seems a little thin, turn the curry into a skillet and simmer until reduced and thick. Taste and add salt if needed.
Makes 4 to 6 servings.

Boiled Beef with Green Sauce
7 to 9 hours

This is a crockery-cooker variation on Bolliti Misti, an Italian dish for those who love the flavor of anchovy and capers. The sauce is made in the blender just before serving.

2 lb. boneless bottom round of beef, cut into 1½-inch cubes	1 large leek, chopped
	1 tsp. salt
	½ tsp. dried thyme
1-lb. piece boneless veal	½ tsp. dried marjoram
10 Italian sausages, hot or sweet	⅛ cup water
1 broiler chicken, quartered	½ cup chopped fresh parsley
1 large onion	2 anchovy fillets
1 clove garlic, peeled and minced	1 tsp. capers
2 large carrots, peeled and coarsely chopped	1 medium clove garlic, peeled and halved
	½ cup olive oil
	1 Tbs. strained lemon juice

To Cook: Place the beef, veal, sausages, chicken, onion, garlic, carrots, leek, salt, thyme, and marjoram in the slow cooker and pour the water over them. Cover and cook on Low for 7 to 9 hours.

Before Serving: Just before serving, combine the remaining ingredients in the recipe in the blender and blend on low until the sauce is smooth. Turn the meats and the cooking juices into a deep serving dish and offer the green sauce in a sauce boat on the side.
Makes 8 to 10 servings.

Beef Stew
8 to 10 hours

⅓ cup all-purpose flour	3 heaping Tbs. tomato paste
¼ tsp. black pepper	½ tsp. salt
½ tsp. celery salt	1 tsp. Worcestershire sauce
1¾ lb. boneless chuck or round beef, cut into 1½-inch cubes	12 small carrots, peeled, or 3 large carrots, peeled and quartered
¼ cup vegetable oil	
1 cup minced onion	4 to 5 medium potatoes, peeled and quartered
3 medium cloves garlic, peeled and minced	
	¼ cup finely minced parsley
1½ cups boiling water	

To Cook: In a large bowl, combine the flour, pepper, and celery salt. Toss the meat in the flour. In a large skillet, over medium-high heat, heat the oil and brown the meat, stirring often, until darkened on all sides. As soon as each piece finishes browning, lift it into a small bowl. When all the meat is done, toss the onion and garlic together in the fat remaining in the skillet. Remove the skillet from the heat. Stir in the leftover flour, then stir in the boiling water, working quickly to keep the sauce smooth. Add the tomato paste, salt, and Worcestershire sauce. Scrape the bottom of the skillet to get up all the pan juices and turn into the slow cooker. Place the carrots and potatoes in the bottom of the cooker and scrape the meat over them. Cover and cook on Low for 8 to 10 hours.
Before Serving: Garnish the finished stew with the parsley.
Makes 4 servings.

Boeuf Bourguignon in Noodle Ring

Boeuf Bourguignon in a Noodle Ring
8 to 10 hours

A treat served in a noodle ring. To make a noodle ring, just cook the noodles as directed on the package and turn them into a ring mold. As they cool, they'll jell into the ring shape, and you can fill the center with the Boeuf Bourguignon.

¼ lb. strip fatty pork, cut into ½-inch pieces	½ tsp. ground thyme
4 lb. boneless chuck or round beef, cut into 2- to 2½-inch cubes	½ tsp. ground savory
	2 Tbs. butter
	1 small onion, peeled and minced
3 Tbs. all-purpose flour	1 lb. mushrooms, wiped clean, caps and stems separated, and cut on a slant
1½ cups dry red wine	
½ cup beef bouillon or ½ cup water with 1 bouillon cube	
	3 cloves garlic, peeled and minced
Salt	4 sprigs parsley, chopped
½ tsp. pepper	
1 bay leaf	

To Cook: In a large skillet, over medium heat, sauté the pork to render the fat. Remove and reserve the pork bits. Raise the heat to high and thoroughly brown the beef pieces, a few at a time. As they finish cooking, lift them into the slow cooker. Remove the skillet from the heat, and stir the flour into the drippings, working rapidly. Stirring all the time, add the wine and the bouillon. The sauce should be as thick as heavy cream; if it isn't, simmer a little longer. Add the salt and pepper, bay leaf, thyme, savory, and pork bits. Make sure you have scraped up all the pan juices and turn the sauce into the cooker. Cover and cook on Low for about 8 hours.

Before Serving: In a medium skillet, over medium-high heat, melt the butter and sauté the onion until translucent. With a slotted spoon, lift the onion bits into the slow cooker. Sauté the mushrooms in the skillet, stirring, for 2 minutes. Add the garlic and parsley. Stir and cook for 1 minute. Skim any visible fat from the cooking liquids in the slow cooker and spoon a little liquid into the skillet. Scrape up the pan juices, then scrape mushrooms and juices back into the slow cooker. Cover and cook for another hour or two.
Makes 10 to 12 servings.

Beef Stew with Zucchini
8 to 10 hours

In mid-season when zucchini comes in, try this recipe for beef stew. Select small, fresh zucchini whose skin is fresh enough to be broken easily with a thumbnail, and don't pare the vegetables. You can use marrow or summer squash instead of zucchini.

2 lb. boneless chuck or stew beef cut into 1½-inch cubes	1 bay leaf
	2 large stalks celery, cut into 2-inch pieces
1 Tbs. vegetable oil	
2 tsp. salt	6 medium potatoes, pared and quartered
¼ tsp. pepper	
1 medium onion, peeled and sliced	2 zucchini, stemmed and cut into 1-inch slices
½ cup water	
¼ tsp. marjoram	2 Tbs. all-purpose flour
1 medium green pepper, seeded and chopped	

Beef Stew with Zucchini

Carbonnades à la Flamande
8 to 10 hours

This is a Belgian dish, beef stewed in beer, and world famous. Serve with it boiled young carrots and boiled quartered potatoes garnished with finely minced parsley. As a substitute for the fresh onions called for here, you may prefer to use ½ cup onion flakes soaked in ⅓ cup water for 10 minutes before using.

3 lb. boneless chuck roast, cut into 2-inch cubes	2 Tbs. firmly packed light brown sugar
½ Tbs. vegetable oil	1½ Tbs. salt
½ Tbs. salt	2 large sprigs fresh parsley or 1 Tbs. dried parsley flakes
1 tsp. pepper	
⅛ cup butter	
4 cups peeled, sliced onions	1 large bay leaf
2 large cloves garlic, peeled and minced	½ tsp. dried thyme
	1½ Tbs. cornstarch
1 can (12 oz.) light beer	2 Tbs. white vinegar

To Cook: In a large skillet, over medium heat, sauté the meat in the oil until well browned on all sides. Remove the meat to a bowl and season with the ½ tablespoon salt and the pepper. In the same skillet, melt the butter and sauté the onions, stirring often, until medium brown in color. A minute before the onions are done, stir in the garlic. Turn the onions and garlic into the slow cooker. Add the browned meat and juices from the bowl on top. To the still hot skillet add the beer, brown sugar, the 1½ tablespoons salt, parsley, bay leaf, and thyme. Scrape up the pan juices and turn into the slow cooker. Cover and cook on Low for 8 to 10 hours.

Before Serving: After the meat is finished, pour the cooking liquid into a measuring cup. If you have more than 2 cups of liquid, cook over high heat in a skillet until the juice is reduced. Thicken these 2 cups of sauce by simmering with cornstarch dissolved in vinegar for 3 to 4 minutes, stirring constantly. Place the onions in the bottom of the serving dish, set the meat cubes on top, and spoon the sauce over all.
Makes 6 to 8 servings.

To Cook: In a large skillet over medium-high heat, thoroughly brown the meat pieces in the oil. Sprinkle half the salt and pepper over the meat. Lift the meat into a bowl. Sauté the onion in the skillet until translucent and lift the onion into the slow cooker. In the still hot skillet, swirl the water, scraping up the pan juices, then turn the liquid into the slow cooker. Add the marjoram, green pepper, bay leaf, celery, potatoes, and zucchini and sprinkle with the remaining salt and pepper. Place the meat on top. Cover and cook on Low for 8 to 10 hours.

Before Serving: Remove the meat and vegetables to a serving platter and keep warm. Skim 1 or 2 tablespoons of fat from the top of the cooking liquid and heat in a medium skillet over medium-low heat. Stir the flour into the fat. Pour the hot cooking liquid over the flour and beat rapidly to make a smooth sauce. Simmer until the sauce is as thick as whipped cream, then pour over the meat and vegetables.
Makes 6 to 8 servings.

Meat Pie
5 to 6 hours; bake crust 20 to 30 minutes

This is one of my favorites for the slow cooker. Because the meat cooks while I'm at work, all I have to do when I get home is add the topping or crust and bake it while I'm preparing vegetables and setting the table.

2 lb. ground beef or leftover meat loaf	1 tsp. dry mustard
	1 Tbs. Tabasco sauce
¼ cup all-purpose flour	6 small white onions, peeled
1½ tsp. salt	1¼ cups water
½ tsp. ground ginger	Bisquick (enough for 10 biscuits) or commercial pie-crust mix (½ recipe)
⅛ tsp. ground cinnamon	
3 Tbs. vegetable oil	

Meat Pie

To Cook: In a medium bowl, combine the flour, salt, ginger, and cinnamon. In a medium skillet, over medium-high heat, brown the meat in the oil quickly, stirring constantly, then mix with the ingredients in the bowl and turn into the slow cooker. Add the mustard, Tabasco sauce, onion, and water. Cover and cook on Low for 5 or 6 hours. (If using leftover meat loaf already seasoned, eliminate the flour and salt.)

Before Serving: If using Bisquick, prepare enough to make 10 biscuits. Turn the cooked meat into a 1½-quart oven-proof casserole. If the sauce seems very thin, simmer a few minutes to thicken it. Scoop biscuit mix in dollops over the meat and bake as directed, about 15 minutes. If using pie crust as a topping, prepare ½ recipe for a two-crust pie. Transfer the meat to a casserole or a deep pie dish 8 to 9 inches in diameter, top with the raw crust, and bake at 425° F. in a preheated oven for 20 to 30 minutes, just long enough to turn the crust a deep gold. If you brush cold milk over the crust, it will brown better.
Makes 6 servings.

Steak and Kidney Pie
5 to 6 hours; bake crust 20 to 30 minutes

This is another of my favorites for the slow cooker.

6 fresh lamb kidneys	3 Tbs. vegetable oil
	1 tsp. dry mustard
¼ cup all-purpose flour	1 Tbs. Worcestershire sauce
1½ tsp. salt	6 small white onions, peeled
½ tsp. ground ginger	1¼ cups water
⅛ tsp. ground cinnamon	Bisquick (enough for 10 biscuits) or commercial pie-crust mix (½ recipe)
1½ lb. boneless beef round, cut into 1-inch cubes	

To Cook: Under cold water, wash the kidneys well, then remove the outer sack and fat and place the kidneys in a very large bowl of ice water. Using scissors, remove remaining fat and tubes from the kidneys. Discard these and cut the kidneys in the ice water into ¼-inch slices. In a medium bowl, combine the flour, salt, ginger, and cinnamon. Drain kidneys. Toss the beef and kidney pieces in the mixture. In a medium skillet, over medium-high heat, brown the meats in the oil quickly, stirring constantly, then turn the meats into the slow cooker. Add the mustard, Worcestershire sauce, onion, and water. Cover and cook on Low for 5 to 6 hours.

Before Serving: Thicken sauce by simmering if necessary and follow pie-crust instructions for Meat Pie. Transfer the meat to the oven-proof casserole or a deep pie dish, top with the raw crust, and bake at 425° F. in a preheated oven for 20 to 30 minutes. Brush cold milk over the crust to make it brown better. Makes 6 servings.

Swiss Steak Jardinière

Swiss Steak Jardinière
6 to 8 hours

This is a variation to play on Swiss steak. It uses mushrooms, fresh or canned.

1½ lb. round or rump steak, cut in slices ½ inch thick	6 medium carrots, peeled and halved
¼ cup all-purpose flour	2 medium green peppers, seeded and cut into 1-inch pieces
1 tsp. salt	
¼ tsp. black pepper	1 lb. fresh mushrooms, rinsed, patted dry, and cut in half, or 2 cans (6 to 8 oz.), drained
2 Tbs. vegetable oil	
½ cup chopped onion	
1 medium clove garlic, peeled and minced	
1½ cups fresh or canned tomatoes, quartered	½ tsp. salt

To Cook: Remove any excess fat from the meat slices and lay them on a cutting board. Sprinkle with half the flour, salt, and pepper.

With the back of a heavy kitchen knife or with the edge of a saucer rim, pound the flour into the meat. Repeat on the other side, using the remaining flour, salt, and pepper. In a large skillet, over medium-high heat, brown the meat slices on each side in the oil, 2 or 3 minutes. Lift the meat into a bowl. Add the onion, garlic, and tomatoes to the still hot skillet, and sauté, scraping up the pan juices, for 2 or 3 minutes. Turn into the slow cooker. Add the carrots and the green peppers, then the meat. Cover and cook on Low for 6 to 8 hours.

Before Serving: Lift the meat and vegetables onto a heated serving platter. Skim the surface of the cooking liquids to gather one or two tablespoons of fat, and turn these into a large skillet. Over medium-high heat, sauté the mushrooms, tossing constantly, until moisture has dried and pieces are tender, about 5 minutes. Add salt. Pour the cooking liquid from the slow cooker over the mushrooms and simmer briefly, scraping up pan juices. Sauce should be the consistency of heavy cream. Pour over meat and vegetables.
Makes 4 to 6 servings.

Braised Short Ribs of Beef
7 to 10 hours

Short ribs are really delicious, as long as they are cooked slowly and at length—and they're among the most inexpensive of beef cuts. This dish may be served on a bed of boiled noodles. A dash of Tabasco sauce peps it up.

2 Tbs. all-purpose flour	5 small white onions, peeled
2 tsp. salt	4 large carrots, scraped and quartered
½ tsp. black pepper	
2 lb. short ribs of beef, cut into 3- to 4-inch pieces	8 stalks celery, cut into 2-inch pieces
2 Tbs. vegetable oil	¾ cup boiling water
4 medium potatoes, pared and halved	

To Cook: In a large bowl, combine the flour, salt, and pepper and toss the meat in it until well coated on all sides. In a large skillet, over medium-high heat, brown the meat in the oil. Remove each piece as soon as it is browned and set in a bowl. Turn the vegetables into the hot skillet, sauté them quickly (2 or 3 minutes), and turn into a bowl. Remove the skillet from the heat and stir in the remaining flour, working quickly to make a smooth paste. Add the boiling water, stirring constantly to smooth the sauce, and scrape the bottom of the skillet to get up all the juices. Turn the sauce into the slow cooker and add the vegetables, then the meat. Cover and cook on Low for 7 to 10 hours. Makes 4 servings.

Marinated Chuck Roast or Brisket of Beef
8 to 10 hours

If your household likes hearty, plain food, try beef brisket this way. It's one of my favorite recipes and ever so easy. The only caution is that the beef must marinate overnight. Serve with parsley potatoes.

3 lb. chuck roast or brisket of beef	1 tsp. Tabasco sauce
2 Tbs. Kitchen Bouquet	⅛ cup lukewarm water

Braised Short Ribs of Beef

To Cook: Place beef in a bowl and spread Kitchen Bouquet and Tabasco on all surfaces. Marinate overnight, covered, in the refrigerator. Remove the meat from the refrigerator as soon as you get up in the morning and allow it 15 or 20 minutes to warm up to room temperature. Add water to the slow cooker, just enough to make about ¼ inch of water in the bottom of the utensil. Add the beef, cover, and cook on Low for 8 to 10 hours.

Before Serving: If the juices in the bottom of the cooker are thin, simmer in a small saucepan over high heat for a few minutes to thicken them. Place the meat on a serving platter, pour the thickened pan juices over, and serve at once.
Makes 5 to 6 servings.

Beef Shank Cross Cut with Vegetables
7 to 9 hours

Beef shank cross cut is an excellent piece of stewing meat. There's lots of cartilage in it, and the slow cooking method is exactly what it needs. Cooked here with vegetables, it makes a fine one-dish dinner.

Marinated Chuck Roast or Brisket of Beef

Beef Shank Cross Cut with Vegetables

3 lb. beef shank cross cut, 1 inch thick
2 Tbs. all-purpose flour
2 tsp. salt
¼ tsp. pepper
1 Tbs. vegetable oil
¼ cup water
1 large sprig parsley
½ tsp. thyme
1 bay leaf
1 small onion, peeled and stuck with 4 whole cloves
3 medium carrots, peeled and cut into pieces 1 inch long
4 large stalks celery, cut in pieces 3 inches long
12 to 15 Brussels sprouts or 1 package (10 oz.) frozen sprouts, cooked (optional)

To Cook: In a large bowl or a plastic bag, toss the meat with the flour combined with the salt and pepper. In a medium skillet, over medium-high heat, heat the oil and brown the meat well on all sides. Remove the meat to a bowl. Pour the water into the still hot skillet and scrape up the pan juices. Turn the liquid into the slow cooker. Add the herbs, onion, carrots, and celery. Place the meat on top. Cover and cook on Low for 7 to 9 hours, or until meat is completely tender.

Before Serving: Cook the Brussels sprouts. Lift the meat and vegetables to a warm serving platter and add sprouts. In a medium skillet, simmer cooking juices until the consistency of heavy cream and pour over the meat and vegetables.
Makes 4 to 6 servings.

Flank Steak Southern Style
8 to 10 hours

Flank steak is a wedge of rather thin beef that comes from the flank of the animal. It is boneless and can be done lots of ways. This way is a favorite, nice with boiled rice.

1 flank steak (about 2 lb.)
2 Tbs. vegetable oil
3 cups sliced onion
1 large clove garlic, peeled and minced
¾ cup ketchup
1 tsp. salt
⅛ tsp. black pepper
⅛ tsp. ground thyme

To Cook: With a sharp knife, lightly slash the surface of the steak. In a large skillet, over high heat, heat the oil and brown the steak quickly on both sides. Remove the skillet from the heat and lift the meat into the slow cooker. At once turn the remaining ingredients into the hot oil and scrape the pan to gather all the juices. Turn the sauce into the cooker, cover and cook on Low for 8 to 10 hours.
Makes 5 to 6 servings.

Cocido

into a bowl. Pour a cupful of the water into the browning skillet while it is still hot and scrape up the pan juices. Turn this liquid into the slow cooker, along with all the other ingredients, and top with the beef. Cover and cook on Low for 8 to 10 hours, or until the chick peas are tender. If the chick peas absorb all the liquid (how they cook depends on their age and a number of other variables) and aren't tender, add half a cupful more of water and continue to cook. Usually there's lots of rich sauce left when the cooking is done.

Before Serving: Remove and discard the ham bone. Dice the meat from the chicken bones into the Cocido, and discard the bones. If the sauce seems thin, pour it into a small skillet and simmer over medium-high heat, stirring, until thickened.

Makes 8 servings.

Cocido
8 to 10 hours

This is an adaptation of a recipe for Spanish Cocido, which is best made with Spanish olive oil, if you have it. It is made with chick peas (garbanzos), leftover ham, and chicken parts — a great dish when economy is an objective. The beans must soak overnight before cooking. You can buy canned garbanzos in many areas. If these are used, do not add the quart of water called for in the recipe below.

¼ cup olive or vegetable oil	2 large tomatoes, stemmed and quartered
2 lb. boneless stew beef, cut into 1½-inch cubes	½ cup minced parsley
1 quart water	1 cup small ham cubes
1 lb. dried chick peas, soaked overnight	1 ham bone
3 large onions, peeled and sliced	4 chicken wings or 2 wings plus neck and backbone
2 medium cloves garlic, peeled and minced	2 tsp. salt
	½ tsp. pepper
	4 medium carrots, peeled and diced

To Cook: In a large skillet, over high heat, heat the oil and brown the beef on all sides. Lift

Slow-Pot Meat Sauce

Slow-Pot Meat Sauce
6 to 8 hours

Meat sauce that has cooked ever so slowly all day is really better than meat sauce made in a hurry. This is great on any of the pastas or baked beans or rice. Offer grated Parmesan cheese with the meat sauce.

3 Tbs. olive oil or vegetable oil	⅔ cup water
1 large onion, peeled and chopped	1 tsp. sugar
	1 tsp. dried basil
	1 tsp. dried oregano
2 large cloves garlic, peeled and minced	2 large green peppers, seeded and chopped
1½ lb. ground beef or hamburger	2 large stalks celery, diced
1 can (16 oz.) whole Italian tomatoes	½ lb. mushrooms, stemmed, or 1 can (10 oz.) mushrooms
1 can (6 oz.) tomato paste	2 tsp. salt
	½ tsp. pepper

To Cook: In a large skillet, over medium-high heat, heat the oil and sauté the onion and the garlic until the onions are well browned but not burned. With a slotted spoon, remove to the slow cooker. Turn the meat into the skillet, break it up, and sauté it on high heat, stirring often until it is in little lumps and well browned. Add the tomatoes, the tomato paste, and the water to the still hot skillet and scrape up the pan juices. Turn off the heat and add the sugar and all the other ingredients to the sauce. Combine well, then stir into the contents of the slow pot. Cover and cook on Low for 6 to 8 hours. The sauce is relatively well cooked after about 4 hours but it will taste best after a longer cooking period.

Before Serving: If the sauce seems a little thin (which it shouldn't), simmer it in a skillet for 4 or 5 minutes before serving.

Makes 3 to 6 servings.

Meat Loaf
5 to 7 hours

This is my family's favorite meat loaf recipe. Use it as a guide to adapt your family meat loaf recipe to slow cooking.

½ cup whole milk or condensed milk	1½ tsp. salt
	½ tsp. pepper
2 slices white bread	1 tsp. dry mustard
1½ lb. ground beef or hamburger	1 can (12 oz.) whole tomatoes
2 eggs	
1 small onion, peeled	

Slow-Pot Meat Loaf

To Cook: Place the milk and bread in a large mixing bowl and allow to sit until the bread has absorbed all the milk. With two forks, break the bread into crumbs. Beat the hamburger into the crumbs until well mixed. Make a hole in the center of the hamburger and break the eggs into it. Beat the eggs a little, then grate the onion into the eggs. Add salt, pepper, and mustard. Beat the eggs into the hamburger. Make a round cake of the meat and place in the slow cooker. Drain the tomatoes and place the whole tomatoes on top of the meat. Cover and cook on Low for 5 to 7 hours.

Before Serving: Uncover the pot, turn the heat to High, and bubble away some of the sauce. It should be thick, not thin.

Makes 6 servings.

Procedure   *Breaking eggs into a well made in the mixed ground beef, bread, and milk. Secret to success with this dish is to keep the beef mixture as light and fluffy as possible.*

Mother's Hamburger Rice Dish
6 to 8 hours

This is a rice, hamburger, onions, and tomato combination that is super simple and tastes terrific.

1½ cups converted rice	1½ cups water
½ cup vegetable oil	1 large onion, chopped
1 lb. hamburger or ground beef	1 large green pepper, seeded and chopped
1 large can whole tomatoes	1½ tsp. salt
1 can (6 oz.) tomato paste	

To Cook: In a medium skillet, sauté the rice over medium heat in the oil until the rice becomes opaque. Remove the rice to the slow cooker. In the same skillet, sauté the hamburger over high heat. Crumble it as you sauté it and let the undersides heat enough to stick and turn brown. Turn the hamburger into the slow pot. Add the tomatoes, tomato paste, and water to the skillet; scrape up the pan juices. Add the onion, green pepper, and salt, then turn the whole contents of the skillet into the cooker. Cover and cook on Low for 6 to 8 hours. Makes 4 to 6 servings.

Meatballs in Mushroom Sauce
4 to 6 hours

1 lb. ground chuck beef	1 cup unflavored bread crumbs
¼ lb. ground pork shoulder	½ cup milk
1 medium onion, peeled and minced	1 can condensed cream of mushroom soup
½ cup raw converted rice	¼ tsp. salt
1 egg, slightly beaten	⅛ tsp. black pepper
1½ tsp. salt	2 tsp. soy sauce or Worcestershire sauce
¼ tsp. black pepper	
⅛ tsp. ground allspice	

To Cook: In a large bowl, combine the beef, pork, onion, rice, egg, the 1½ teaspoons salt, the ¼ teaspoon pepper, allspice, and milk.

Shape the mixture into balls about the size of a golf ball. In the slow cooker, combine the soup, the ¼ teaspoon salt, the ⅛ teaspoon pepper, and soy sauce or Worcestershire sauce. Add the meatballs and mix quickly. Cover and cook on Low for 4 to 6 hours.
Makes 6 servings.

Chili con Carne
5 to 7 hours

This is a meaty variation on Mexican chili sauce. It's hot, and I combine it with rice. It can be made from very lean chuck or from hamburger. If you make it with hamburger, skim away any excess fat from the sauce before serving.

1 lb. lean ground chuck beef or hamburger	1½ Tbs. chili powder
	½ tsp. salt
1 cup chopped onion	1 can (7½ oz.) whole tomatoes
1 large clove garlic, peeled and minced	⅔ cup tomato puree
	1 cup drained canned red kidney beans
1 tsp. oregano	
¼ tsp. pepper	4 cups hot cooked rice
1 tsp. ground cumin	

To Cook: Place all the ingredients except the beans and cooked rice in the slow cooker, cover, and cook on Low for 5 to 7 hours. Before you begin to cook the rice, drain and measure the beans and mix into the chili sauce; then continue the cooking.

Before Serving: If the sauce seems thin after the cooking is finished, pour it into a small skillet and simmer over medium heat until thick. Pour over the chili and serve with hot cooked rice on the side.
Makes 6 servings.

Veal

Most veal slow-cook recipes give you 5 to 7 hours of free time. Veal is beef before it grows up. Like beef, it is a dense meat. A veal roast is delicious, if a little dense, and tender, but it does not often appear on my supermarket menu — it's expensive meat. It stands to

Chili Con Carne

2 lb. boned veal shoulder, cut in 2-inch pieces	1 lb. (about 15) small white onions, peeled
1 quart water	½ lb. small fresh mushrooms, wiped and stemmed
1 small onion, peeled and stuck with 4 whole cloves	
5 scraped carrots, quartered	2 Tbs. butter
1 bay leaf	¼ cup all-purpose flour
⅛ tsp. dried thyme	2 egg yolks
½ cup diced celery	2 Tbs. strained lemon juice
4 peppercorns	
1 tsp. salt	1 Tbs. minced parsley
¼ cup butter	

To Cook: In the slow cooker, place the veal, water, onion, carrots, bay leaf, thyme, celery, peppercorns, and salt. Cover and cook on Low for 4 to 6 hours.

Before Serving: When the veal has finished cooking, or about ¾ of an hour before you intend to serve dinner, melt ¼ cup butter in medium skillet, turn the onions into the butter, and cover. Simmer at low heat for 25 minutes, or until the onions are cooked through. Don't let the onions color (they will if the heat is too high). Remove the onions to a warm serving dish. In the same skillet, sauté the mushroom caps, uncovered, for 5 minutes and scoop them into the serving dish. Melt 2 tablespoons butter in the skillet over low heat, stir in the flour, measure 3½ cups of the veal cooking liquid into the skillet, and stir quickly to make a smooth sauce. Place the egg yolks in a cup, beat slightly, mix in the lemon juice, and stir in ¼ cup of the hot sauce. Stir this back into the skillet of sauce. Heat, without boiling, for 3 or 4 minutes. Lift the veal and vegetables from the slow cooker, drain well, and turn into the serving dish. Pour the sauce over the meat, garnish with parsley, and serve. If you reheat this dish at any point, don't let it boil.
Makes 6 to 8 servings.

reason that it usually is better business to let a calf grow up to become a lot of meat for sale.

Boned veal shoulder, however, often is offered at a reasonable price and it makes excellent casseroles and stews. It doesn't require as lengthy cooking as beef; 4 to 6 hours, in my experience, is enough to completely cook boned veal shoulder cut into 2-inch pieces.

If boned veal shoulder comes your way often at a good price, select from among the many beef casserole recipes in the preceding section. Veal is a more subtly flavored meat than beef, so choose low-key casseroles rather than strongly flavored dishes. Veal is particularly good with tomatoes.

Blanquette de Veau
4 to 6 hours

Veal is a luxury meat, and not one, as a rule, that benefits from lots and lots of cooking. However, you can make this veal casserole in your slow cooker. The second step — cooking the onions and mushrooms and making the

Osso Bucco
8 to 10 hours

This dish is best when cooked slowly until the meat falls off the bones, and a slow cooker is the best utensil to cook it in. Since the delicacy here is the marrow in the bone, select young veal shanks. They should weigh about 1½ pounds each. Serve Gremolata Sauce on the side — if your family approves of garlic.

¼ cup all-purpose flour
½ tsp. salt
¼ tsp. pepper
6 lb. veal shanks, cut into 2-inch pieces
½ cup oil
1 medium onion, peeled and minced
1 medium carrot, scraped and minced
1 stalk celery, minced

2 cloves garlic, peeled and minced
½ cup dry white wine
½ cup beef bouillon or ½ cup water with 1 bouillon cube
1 can (12 oz.) whole tomatoes, drained and chopped
½ tsp. basil
½ tsp. rosemary
Gremolata Sauce (optional)

To Cook: Mix the flour, salt, and pepper in a large bowl and toss the veal shanks in the mixture until well coated. In a large skillet, heat half the oil over medium-high heat. A few pieces at a time, brown the veal on all sides until deeply colored and crusty looking. In another skillet, over medium heat, sauté the onion, carrot, celery, and garlic in the oil that remains, for 3 to 4 minutes. Turn the vegetables into the slow cooker. Arrange the veal on top; stand it so the marrow will stay inside the bone when it begins to tenderize. Pour the wine into one of the skillets and scrape up the pan juices. Pour the bouillon into the other skillet and scrape up the pan juices. Pour wine and bouillon over the ingredients in the slow cooker and add the drained tomatoes, basil, and rosemary. Cover and cook on Low for 8 to 10 hours.

Before Serving: If the sauce seems thin, simmer in a skillet until thickened. Check seasonings and add salt and pepper if needed. Makes 6 to 8 servings.

Gremolata Sauce

6 cloves garlic, peeled and minced
2 Tbs. grated lemon peel

½ cup chopped fresh parsley

Combine all the ingredients, and mix well. Serve on the side with Osso Bucco.

Veal Curry

Follow the recipe for Simple Beef Curry (page 28), but use 1 pound of cubed veal instead of beef.

4
Pork and Ham

Pork and ham slow-cook recipes give you 8 to 12 hours of free time. The slow cooker is, in my opinion, ideal for cooking some pork products and not ideal for others. It's great for ham in sizes small enough to fit in your cooker. Ham is superb when cooked very slowly; as far as I am concerned, the slow cooker can do no wrong with ham. I haven't had the same luck with all pork cuts. Pork should be cooked slowly, too, but I have found that loin and end of loin roasts (the rib section of the pork) really are better slowly roasted rather than slowly cooked in an electric crockery pot. The slow pot just doesn't do much for them. The meat seems to get tough and stringy.

The slow pot does do superbly all manner of pork chops. As you know, pork chops — unlike most other chops — are hard to cook through without drying out. The slow cooker eliminates all that, cooks the chops all day, and turns them out falling-off-the-bone tender and sweet. I've cooked pork chops with nothing added to the slow pot but a little beef bouillon, and found them delicious. However, it's worth the trouble to add a few other ingredients and make the chops into a casserole with a gravy. Though pork doesn't resemble beef, a number of the flavorful beef casserole recipes can be used with pork chops. Buy small chops, remove the excess fat, and cook them whole or halved rather than cut into 2- or 2½-inch pieces, as called for in the beef recipes.

Pork hocks appear occasionally in my supermarket, and they're among the specialty meats that a slow cooker really does wonders with. Adapt your own favorite pork-hock recipes following the timing described in the recipe that follows.

Sausages and really fatty pork products should be sautéed to remove most of the fat if they are to be slow cooked alone. If fat is a large part of the content, the meat ends up cooking for hours in fat and this doesn't make them ideal candidates for slow cooking — with some exceptions. There are bean dishes and other casseroles in which sausages make the dish. I've included a few in this book. Stuffed Cabbage Catalan calls for ground pork (which is like spicy sausage meat) and the New England Boiled Dinner includes a Polish sausage (but any large, flavorful German sausage will do — except knockwurst, which duplicates the flavor of the corned beef in the recipe), and Cassoulet, which is made with beans, calls for a garlic sausage.

Slow-Cooked Pork Chops

Slow-Cooked Pork Chops
8 to 10 hours

This is a two-step recipe. You do all the work at the beginning and can let the dish cook almost indefinitely after that. I offer fresh sour cream on the side with this. To dress up the dish, boiled potatoes and braised celery may be added before serving.

12 to 16 small pork chops	½ tsp. pepper
6 large Bermuda or sweet onions, peeled and thickly sliced	¾ cup chicken broth or 1 cup water with Steero chicken granules
2 tsp. salt	1 tsp. chopped chives (optional)

To Cook: Trim any extra fat from the chops and, in a large skillet over high heat, melt down the fat and discard the bits of pork. Turn the heat to medium and sauté the onions in the fat until translucent. Keep the rounds intact if you can. Remove the onions to a bowl. Turn the heat to medium high and brown all of the pork well on both sides; keep meat in the skillet only long enough to brown, for 3 or 4 minutes. Salt and pepper the pork and remove to a bowl. Turn the heat off, add the broth to the skillet, and scrape up the pan juices. In the slow cooker, beginning with onions, layer the pork and the onions, ending with onions. Pour the broth over all, cover, and cook on Low for 8 to 10 hours.
Makes 8 to 12 servings.

Slow-Cooked Bavarian Pork
10 to 12 hours

The slow pot is a great asset in preparing this Pennsylvania dish, since the hocks must cook for hours before being finished in an oven.

2 to 3 lb. fresh pork hocks (6 to 8)	¼ tsp. pepper
	About 4 cups water
2 large onions, peeled	2 green apples, cored
1 bay leaf	3 lb. sauerkraut
2 celery stalks, diced	½ cup light brown sugar, firmly packed
2½ tsp. salt	

To Cook: Place the hocks, onions, bay leaf, celery, salt, pepper, and water to cover in the slow cooker. Cover and cook on Low for 10 to 12 hours, or until the hocks are thoroughly cooked.
Before Serving: Turn the oven to 325° F. Remove the hocks from the cooker and place in a small casserole, closely packed. Cut the apples into wedges and place them over the hocks. Cover both with sauerkraut, not drained, and sprinkle with the brown sugar. Bake in the preheated oven for ¾ hour.
Makes 6 to 8 servings.

New England Boiled Dinner
6 to 8 hours

This is a favorite of my family's, simple but hearty, and just right for cold winter nights. Since the crockery cooker does most of the work, I can start it in the morning and serve it for supper when I get home. I serve prepared mustard and butter for the vegetables with this.

1 Polish sausage	½ tsp. dried marjoram
4 large potatoes, peeled and halved	½ tsp. dried thyme
2 medium carrots, scraped and cut in rounds	1 onion, peeled and stuck with 4 cloves
1 stalk celery, sliced in rounds	1 tsp. chopped fresh parsley or ½ tsp. parsley flakes
1½ to 2 lb. piece of corned beef	1 tsp. caraway seeds (optional)
3 cups sauerkraut, drained and rinsed	Water to cover, about 3 cups

To Cook: Place the sausage in the bottom of the slow cooker and layer the vegetables, except the sauerkraut, on top. Place the corned beef next and cover it with sauerkraut. Combine the spices and the water and pour into the crockery cooker; it should reach a level just below the kraut. Sprinkle the kraut with caraway seeds, if desired, cover, and cook on Low for 6 to 8 hours.

Before Serving: Lift the ingredients gently from the cooker and arrange attractively on a large platter. Moisten with a little of the cooking liquid.

Makes 6 to 8 servings.

Pork Curry

Follow the recipe for Simple Beef Curry (page 28), but use 1 pound of cubed pork instead of beef.

Stuffed Cabbage Catalan
5 to 7 hours

Leftover chicken or ham is used to stuff the cabbage in this recipe, and the whole is cooked in white wine or, if you want to really go overboard, in champagne. You will get a different flavor but an excellent dish by substituting light beer for the wine. Use College Inn chicken bouillon or bouillon made with Steero granules.

1 medium leafy green cabbage	1 medium onion, peeled and sliced
½ lb. fresh ground pork	4 carrots, scraped and diced
½ cup cooked, minced chicken or ham	1 bay leaf
	½ tsp. dried thyme
1 medium onion, peeled and minced	4 whole cloves
	8 whole peppercorns
1 tsp. salt	½ cup dry white wine or champagne
¼ tsp. pepper	
⅛ tsp. allspice	½ cup chicken bouillon
2 slices bread, crusts removed, soaked in ½ cup milk	

To Cook: Place the cabbage head in boiling water for a minute. Drain and let cool. In a bowl, mix together the pork, chicken or ham, onion, salt, pepper, allspice, and bread. Place the cabbage on a cutting board and part the leaves gently until you reach the center. Working from the center outward, spread a little of the stuffing on each leaf, pressing each back into place until the cabbage resumes its original shape. Then tie it with a string toward the top. Place the sliced onions, carrots, bay leaf, thyme, cloves, and peppercorns in the bottom of the crockery cooker and set the stuffed cabbage on top. Pour the wine mixed with chicken bouillon over the top, cover, and cook on Low for 5 to 7 hours, or until the cabbage is tender. Remove the string and the bay leaf and peppercorns before serving.

Makes 6 to 8 servings.

Ham in Cider
8 to 10 hours

Slow cookers do ham wonderfully — and all that long cooking can take place while you are away. However, not all the cookers are large enough to handle the average ham, half ham, or even smaller cuts. Measure the diameter of your cooker, and with the figure in mind, go shopping for a ham that fits. Then try this.

Ham that fits your cooker	1 cup brown sugar
	2 tsp. dry mustard
Sweet cider or apple juice to cover (about 4 cups)	1 tsp. ground cloves
	2 cups white seedless raisins

To Cook: Place the ham and the cider in the slow cooker, and cook on Low for 8 to 10 hours.

Before Serving: Remove the ham from the cider. Turn the oven to 375° F. Make a paste of the sugar, mustard, cloves, and a little of the hot cider. A scant tablespoon usually moistens the paste. Remove the outer skin from the ham, if there is one, and smear the ham with the paste. Place the ham in a baking pan and pour in a cupful of the cider cooked in the slow cooker, along with the raisins. Place the pan in the preheated oven and bake half an hour, or just until the paste has turned into a glaze. The cider will have reduced enough to make a flavorful raisin sauce.

The number of servings depends on the size ham your cooker can handle.

Cassoulet
20 to 24 hours

A French version of baked beans, this is a great dish for a party. Cook the beans overnight in the slow cooker; then you can begin to put the dish together in the morning.

4 oz. salt pork	2 lb. boneless
4 cups dried white	shoulder of lamb,
beans	cut into 2-inch
12 cups water	cubes (save the
1 bay leaf	bones)
1 tsp. dried thyme	2 onions, peeled and
4 peppercorns	chopped
2 medium carrots,	2 cloves garlic,
scraped and	peeled and minced
halved	1 cup tomato puree
1 medium onion,	1 big garlic sausage
peeled and stuck	1 cup beef bouillon
with 8 cloves	or 1 cup water and
2 tsp. salt	1½ bouillon cubes
2 Tbs. vegetable oil	1 cup unflavored
2 lb. boneless pork	bread crumbs
loin, cut into	Salt
2-inch cubes (save	Freshly ground black
the bones)	pepper

To Cook: The night before the dish is to be cooked, cover the salt pork with water, bring to a boil, and simmer for 5 minutes; then drain and dice. Place it in the slow cooker, along with the beans, water, bay leaf, thyme, peppercorns, carrots, onion stuck with cloves, and 2 teaspoons of salt. Cover and let cook on Low until morning. In the morning, remove the bay leaf, peppercorns, onion, and any remaining water. In a large skillet, brown the pork and lamb cubes and the bones in the oil. Stir in the chopped onions and garlic and cook 2 minutes. Stir in the tomato puree. Prick the sausage all over with a fork and brown in another skillet. Remove the sausage to a paper towel and cut into ½-inch slices. Place the bones in the bottom of the slow cooker. Combine the meat cubes and the cooked beans. Taste and add salt and pepper to suit your needs. In the cooker, alternate layers of beans and meat mixture with sausage slices, ending with a layer of sausage slices. Pour the beef bouillon over all and top with bread crumbs and a grinding of fresh pepper. Cover and cook on Low for 8 to 10 hours. Remove the bones before serving.
Makes 12 to 16 servings.

Slow-Cooked Daisy Ham Roll
8 to 10 hours

The slow cooker is a great way to handle a daisy roll. Discard the cooking stock or do as I do — use it to make pea soup. Serve the sliced ham with prepared mustard on the side and offer boiled new potatoes and butter with it.

1 daisy ham roll	1 stalk celery,
Water to cover	washed and bro-
1 small onion, peeled	ken into chunks
and stuck	½ tsp. dried thyme
with 4 cloves	2 large sprigs fresh
8 peppercorns	parsley or 1 tsp.
1 bay leaf	dried parsley
1 carrot, broken into	
chunks	

To Cook: Remove the plastic casing from the ham roll. Place all the ingredients in the slow-cook pot, cover, and cook on Low for 8 to 10 hours. Remove the cotton mesh from the roll before serving.
Makes 4 to 6 servings.

Southern Ham Pot
6 to 8 hours

This is a very basic recipe for flavorful ham cooked the slow way.

¼ cup all-purpose	1 large Bermuda
flour	onion, sliced in
2 tsp. salt	rings ½ inch thick
1 tsp. curry powder	1 package (10 oz.)
2 lb. boneless raw	frozen green peas
ham, cut into	¼ cup stuffed green
1-inch cubes	olives, sliced in
6 medium sweet	rings
potatoes, peeled	1 cup boiling water
and cut into slices	2 Tbs. butter
¼ inch thick	

To Cook: In a large bowl, combine the flour, salt, and curry powder and toss the ham cubes in the mixture. Place one-third of the ham cubes in the bottom of the slow cooker and cover with a layer of half the sweet potato slices, the onions, peas, and olives. Repeat these two layers and end with a third layer of ham cubes. Pour the boiling water over the ingredients and dot with butter. Cover and cook on Low 6 to 8 hours until ham is tender.
Makes 6 servings.

5
Chicken, Lamb, and Other Meats

Most chicken slow-cook recipes give you 5 to 7 hours of free time. Chicken cooks more quickly than most foods that are categorized as meats and is not a food that inherently requires electric crock cooking to come up perfect. In the oven, you can bake an average roasting chicken in somewhere around two hours, while split broilers can be readied in less than an hour. However, the slow cooker is a tremendous help in speeding the preparation of chicken casseroles.

To make Chicken à la King with conventional cooking utensils, you'll have to be at or near the stove for an hour or two. The dish doesn't require two hours of hard work; but it does require that specific things be done at specific times. Their sum total keeps you near the stove for a couple of hours. With the slow cooker, you can set the chicken to cook, leave for 5 to 7 hours, and finish the dish about half an hour before meal time. Chicken Cacciatore, a wonderful Italian way with chicken, is made over a period of more than an hour during which various ingredients are added to the cooking pot in sequence. When you are making Chicken Cacciatore in a slow pot, you brown the chicken in a skillet, add it to the slow cooker with the ingredients of the sauce, cook it in your absence, then finish it off with a few sautéed mushroom slices just before serving. Coq au Vin (chicken cooked with wine), a famous gourmet dish from France, is made at about the same rhythm.

You can do chicken plain in a slow pot, too, as described in the recipe just below, Slow-Cooked Chicken Stuffed with Celery. Everything goes into the pot at once with no advance preparation, and it's ready to eat 5 to 7 hours later. Use its timing to create your own favorite variations on the chicken theme. The dish requires no liquid: The celery and the chicken itself provide all the juices necessary to keep the ingredients moist as they cook. Some slow cookers require some liquid be placed in the pot before any cooking takes place. Follow instructions and plan to thicken the sauce when cooking is over, as described earlier.

Can you overcook a chicken in a slow cooker? Yes, you can, but it will still be pretty good. Overcooked chicken generally is stringy and dry when it has been overbaked, but in a casserole recipe done in a slow cooker a chicken can overcook by quite a bit without getting dry and without seeming unpleasantly stringy. I have heard that a test-kitchen chef working with a slow cooker forgot a chicken in the electric crockery cooker for 30 hours and still found it edible — if not exactly up to Cordon Bleu standards.

Chicken and Beans

Chicken with Beans
4 to 6 hours

To make this variation on Blanquette de Veau (page 39), use 2 pounds of chicken pieces, with the bone in, in place of the veal. If you are in the mood for savings, skim chicken fat from the cooking broth for use in place of butter in making the sauce. Use 1 cup of 1-inch celery chunks, ½ cup of leftover white beans and ½ cup of cooked baby limas in place of the mushrooms.

Red Cooked Chicken
7 to 9 hours

For this variation on Walter Fischman's Red Beef Appetizer (page 24), substitute 1½ pounds boned chicken breast for the beef top round.

Slow-Cooked Chicken with Celery
5 to 7 hours

When you want chicken ready to eat the minute you get home, try it this way in your slow cooker. For variety, cook the chicken with fresh basil or tarragon or tomatoes or sliced onions.

3 lb. chicken, cut in quarters or pieces	1 tsp. salt
½ tsp. curry powder	¼ tsp. pepper
1 small bunch celery, cut into 2-inch lengths (save the leaves)	½ tsp. savory
	2 Tbs. all-purpose flour (optional)

To Cook: Wash and wipe the chicken and rub the skin all over with the curry powder. In the bottom of the slow cooker, make a bed of the celery pieces. Place the chicken in the pot, layered with celery leaves, and sprinkle with salt, pepper, and savory. Cover and cook on Low for 5 to 7 hours.

Before Serving: You can serve the chicken plain or you can turn the cooking liquids into a delicious sauce. Drain the juices from the cooker and skim off and reserve about 1 to 2 tablespoons of chicken fat. Pour the cooking juices into a small skillet, turn the heat to high, and boil down until there is ½ to ¾ cup of stock left. In another skillet, over low heat, warm the chicken fat, and stir the flour into it. When you have a smooth paste, pour the cooked-down stock into the skillet, stirring quickly to keep the sauce smooth. Simmer for 3 or 4 minutes, or until thickened. Taste and add salt and pepper if needed. Place the chicken in a serving dish with the celery pieces around the sides and pour the sauce over all.
Makes 6 to 8 servings.

Chicken Pot Pie
5 to 7 hours

This recipe makes an elegant chicken pie. Freeze extra broth; you'll find lots of uses for it in the recipes in this book.

3 lb. chicken, quartered	¼ tsp. thyme
3 small carrots, peeled and cut into 1-inch chunks	2 tsp. salt
	8 peppercorns
	1 cup water
½ cup diced celery	2 Tbs. flour
1 small onion, peeled and stuck with 4 cloves	⅓ cup dry sherry
1 bay leaf	Bisquick (enough for 10 biscuits) or commercial pie-crust mix (½ recipe)

Chicken Pot Pie

To Cook: Into the slow cooker put the chicken, carrots, celery, onion stuck with cloves, bay leaf, thyme, salt, peppercorns, and water. Cover and cook on Low for 5 to 7 hours.

Before Serving: Remove the chicken to a bowl to cool. Skim ⅓ cup of fat from the top of the cooking broth (if there's not enough, add butter). Place the fat in a medium skillet over medium-low heat. Stir the flour into the fat to make a smooth paste and pour over it all at once 1 cup of hot broth. Beat the broth into the flour, working quickly to make a smooth sauce, and simmer, stirring, for 3 to 4 minutes. Stir in the sherry and simmer another minute. You will have a thick sauce. Skin and bone the chicken and cut the meat into chunks about 1 inch square. Place the chicken and the drained carrots and celery in the bottom of a deep 9-inch pie tin or in a 1½-quart shallow casserole. Pour the sauce over them. If using Bisquick, prepare enough to make 10 biscuits. Scoop Bisquick mix in dollops over the meat and bake as directed on the package, about 15 minutes. If using pie crust as a topping, prepare half the recipe for a two-crust pie, top the chicken with the raw crust, and bake at 425° F. in a preheated oven for 20 to 30 minutes, just long enough to cook the pie crust through and turn it to a deep gold. Brush cold milk over the crust before baking it to make the color better. Makes 6 to 8 servings.

Chicken à la King
5 to 7 hours

This is a two-step dish. The slow cooker will ready the chicken while you are away, and you can finish the sauce just before serving. If you have leftover chicken broth, freeze it for future use in cooking.

3 lb. chicken, quartered	⅓ cup dry sherry
8 small onions, peeled	1 large canned pimiento, cut into 1-inch pieces
1 bay leaf	2 Tbs. butter
2 tsp. salt	½ lb. fresh mushrooms, wiped clean, or 1 can (10 oz.) mushrooms, sliced
2 tsp. pepper	
1 cup water	
⅓ cup all-purpose flour	
1 cup light cream or whole milk	½ tsp. salt

To Cook: Into the slow cooker put the chicken, onions, bay leaf, 2 teaspoons of salt, pepper, and water. Cover and cook on Low for 5 to 7 hours.

Before Serving: Remove the chicken to a bowl to cool. Skim ⅓ cup fat from the top of the cooking liquid (if you can't get that much fat from the broth, use butter to make up the difference). Place the fat in a medium skillet over medium-low heat. Stir the flour into the fat to make a smooth paste and pour over it all at once 1 cup of hot chicken broth. Beat the broth into the flour, working quickly to keep the sauce smooth, and simmer, stirring, for 3 or 4 minutes. Stir in the cream or milk and the sherry, and simmer for another minute or two. Add the pimientos. In another skillet, over medium-high heat, sauté the mushroom slices in the butter for about 5 minutes, or until all the moisture has gone from the skillet and the mushrooms are tender. Salt the mushrooms. Skin and bone the chicken and cut the meat into large chunks. Place them in a warm serving dish. Add the mushrooms and the onions and pour the cream sauce over all.
Makes 6 to 8 servings.

Chicken Cacciatore
4 to 5 hours

This is a favorite Italian dish. Serve it with spaghetti. I usually offer grated Parmesan cheese on the side, though that isn't the way it is served by most Italians.

3 lb. chicken, in pieces	1 Tbs. chopped parsley
2 cup olive oil or vegetable oil	1 tsp. salt
	¼ tsp. pepper
2 medium large onions, peeled and chopped	1 tsp. dried basil
	¼ cup dry red wine
2 large cloves garlic, peeled and minced	½ cup sliced fresh mushrooms or 1 can (4½ oz.) mushrooms, sliced
2 8-oz. cans tomato sauce	¼ tsp. salt

To Cook: In large skillet, over medium-high heat, sauté the chicken pieces in the oil until well browned on all sides. Remove the pieces to the slow cooker. Add the onion, garlic, tomato sauce, parsley, 1 teaspoon salt, pepper, basil, and wine to the skillet. Stir to scrape up the pan juices and pour the sauce over the chicken. Cover and cook on Low for 4 to 5 hours.

Before Serving: Remove the chicken pieces to a warm serving dish. Skim 2 or 3 table-spoons of fat from the top of the cooking liquid and place it in a medium skillet. Over medium-high heat, sauté the mushroom slices until tender and the moisture has dried from the skillet. Salt the mushrooms and place with the chicken. Pour the cooking liquids into the skillet and simmer rapidly, stirring often, until the sauce has become very thick. Pour over the chicken and serve.
Makes 6 to 8 servings.

Chicken Wings Marcel
4 to 5 hours

This is a family recipe. It is easy to make, once the chicken is cooked, and that's where the slow cooker is a great help. It must be served the very minute it is finished. If you are planning to serve it to guests, have everything ready to pop into the skillet; just before the guests sit down to the table, finish the cooking. Use the leftover chicken broth to make chicken

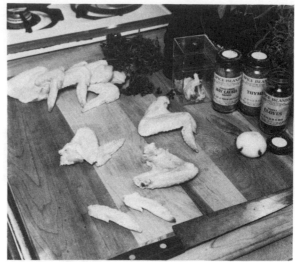

Chicken Wings Marcel   *Wing tips are cut from chicken wings in preparation for the first step in making this dish.*

soup or freeze it in one-cup lots and use it for cooking. The parsley for this must be fresh; don't used dried flakes.

18 chicken wings	3 large sprigs fresh parsley
Water to cover, about 3 or 4 cups	2 tsp. salt
1 small onion, peeled and stuck with 4 cloves	4 Tbs. butter
	1 cup finely minced fresh parsley
1 bay leaf	2 large cloves garlic, peeled and finely minced
½ tsp. dried thyme	
Peppercorns	

To Cook: Cut the wing tips (the skinny bony section) off and place with larger wing pieces in the slow pot, along with enough water to cover them, the onion stuck with cloves, bay leaf, thyme, peppercorns, parsley sprigs, and salt. Cover and cook on Low for 4 to 5 hours.

Before Serving: You can allow the chicken wings to sit in the cooking liquid for an hour or two before you finish the dish, as long as you turn the heat off and remove the cover. Drain the wings, discard the wing tips, and place the wings near the stove. Set a large skillet (the biggest you have) over medium-high heat and melt the butter in it. As soon as it is melted and before it begins to color, add the chicken wings and sauté each to golden brown. Keep them all in the skillet, all browning evenly; it will take 4 to 5 minutes. The dish is especially nice if the

wings crisp a little as they color. Add the garlic and sprinkle the minced parsley over the skillet. With a spatula, toss and sauté the wings with the parsley and garlic, working quickly. In all, this phase should take about 2 minutes — just long enough for the parsley to turn bright green and the dish to give off a strong odor of garlic. Serve the wings the minute they are finished.
Makes 6 servings.

Coq au Vin
7 to 9 hours

The flavor of this French classic is very rich, so plan to serve it with plain-cooked vegetables and a light dessert.

12 small white onions, peeled	1 bay leaf
1 4-lb. roasting chicken, cut up, or 4 lb. chicken thighs	1½ cups dry, strong red wine
	5 Tbs. all-purpose flour
½ tsp. salt	1 cup chicken bouillon
¼ tsp. black pepper	¾ lb. fresh mushrooms, wiped and stemmed
¼ cup brandy or cognac	
2 cloves garlic, peeled and crushed	1 Tbs. butter
	¼ tsp. salt
¼ tsp. ground thyme	1 Tbs. chopped fresh parsley

To Cook: Place onions in the slow cooker. Remove the fat from the vent of the chicken (or cut bits of fat from the chicken thighs) and dice it. In a large skillet, over medium heat, heat the diced fat until all the fat is rendered. Discard the shriveled bits and sauté the chicken pieces in the skillet until well browned. Season with ½ teaspoon salt and ¼ teaspoon pepper. Warm the brandy in a ladle or a small saucepan, set it on fire, and poor it over the chicken. When the flames die, lift the chicken into the slow cooker and add the garlic, thyme, and bay leaf. Pour the wine into the hot skillet and scrape up the pan juices. Dissolve the flour in chicken bouillon, turn into the skillet, and bring to simmering, stirring briskly to avoid lumps. Turn into the slow cooker, cover, and cook on Low for 7 to 9 hours.

Before Serving: About 10 minutes before serving, in a medium skillet, sauté the mushrooms in the butter over medium-high heat. In about 5 minutes, the mushrooms will be tender, and the moisture will have evaporated from the skillet. Season the mushrooms with ¼ teaspoon salt and add to the chicken casserole. If the sauce in the casserole seems thin, simmer it in the mushroom skillet long enough to thicken to the consistency of heavy cream. Garnish the Coq au Vin with parsley before serving.
Makes 8 to 10 servings.

Lamb

Stew lamb done in a slow cooker will free you for about 8 to 10 hours. Leg of lamb isn't a good candidate for the slow cooker. Just look at the shape of a leg of lamb and at the shape of a slow cooker, and you'll see they don't belong together. However, boned lamb shoulder is one of the most delicate of stewing meats, and the slow cooker does it to perfection.

Fitting the Pot   *Leg of lamb is one of the bone-in cuts of meat that can't be fitted into a slow pot. No loss, since this cut of meat is much better roasted or baked than slow-cooked. The slow pot does do wonders, however, for recipes calling for boned lamb shoulder and other lesser cuts of lamb.*

The recipe for Irish Stew, which is traditionally made with lamb, is typical of the way my family handles lamb for stewing. We've learned to be leery of lamb, which often turns out to be mutton. Mutton is grown-up lamb, and the meat is a little redder than lamb, which usually is pinkish. However, you can't always tell one from the other. Mutton has a much stronger flavor than lamb. By blanching the "lamb" for a few minutes in boiling water and discarding the water, you get rid of the strong muttonish flavor. It's a good practice for all lamb-stew packages, unless you know the butcher and are sure the meat will be from a young animal. Blanching isn't necessary — or as necessary — for casseroles or stews that are more strongly seasoned. I've omitted the blanching move in the Navarin Printanier. My theory is that this is a recipe for early spring when the lamb that appears on the market is usually young.

Moussaka
5 to 7 hours

A good way to use cooked leftover lamb. Or use instead raw, ground lamb or even ground round steak, sautéed until brown in 1 or 2 tablespoons olive oil.

5 lb. small eggplants	⅛ tsp. pepper
¼ tsp. cornstarch	2 tsp. salt
¼ cup beef bouillon or ⅓ cup water with Steero beef granules	½ tsp. dried thyme
	½ tsp. dried rosemary
2 Tbs. olive oil	1 small clove garlic, peeled and crushed
2½ cups ground cooked lamb	3 Tbs. tomato paste
⅔ cup minced onions, sautéed in 1 Tbs. olive oil	3 large eggs, well beaten

To Cook: Cut the eggplants in half lengthwise and bake in the oven at 350° F. until tender, about 30 minutes. Scoop the meat into a large mixing bowl and discard the skins. Dissolve the cornstarch in the beef bouillon and beat it, along with the remaining ingredients, into the eggplant pulp. Turn into the slow cooker, cover, and cook on Low for 5 to 7 hours.
Makes 6 to 8 servings.

Lamb Curry
Follow the recipe for Simple Beef Curry (page 28), but use 1 pound of cubed boneless lamb shoulder instead of beef.

Lamb Omar Khayyam with Peanut Ring Mold

Lamb Omar Khayyam
8 to 10 hours

This is an adaptation of a recipe devised by the Wheat Flour Institute. Try it sometime when you want something different. Prepare the Peanut Ring Mold (following) or serve the lamb with rice.

2 lb. boneless lamb shoulder, cut into 2-inch cubes	⅓ cup tomato paste
	1 Tbs. Worcestershire sauce
1 Tbs. vegetable oil	1 tsp. salt
1 carton (8 oz.) plain yogurt	1 tsp. curry powder
	1 bay leaf
½ cup chicken bouillon or ½ cup water with Steero chicken granules	½ cup white wine
	2 Tbs. flour
¼ cup white wine	Peanut Ring Mold (see below)

To Cook: In a large skillet, over medium-high heat, brown the lamb cubes in the oil, then remove the cubes to the slow cooker. Remove the skillet from the heat and add the yogurt, bouillon, ¼ cup wine, tomato paste,

Worcestershire sauce, salt, curry powder, and bay leaf to the skillet. Scrape up the pan juices and turn the sauce into the slow cooker. Cover and cook on Low for 8 to 10 hours.

Before Serving: In a small saucepan, boil the ½ cup of wine until reduced by half. Cool quickly with an ice cube, discard the cube, and and stir the flour into the wine. Remove the lamb cubes from the cooker to a warm serving dish. Turn the cooker to High, stir in the flour and wine, and cook until the sauce has thickened. Combine with the lamb and spoon into a Peanut Ring Mold.
Makes 6 servings.

Peanut Ring Mold

4 cups enriched bread cubes	½ cup chopped celery
⅓ cup chopped peanuts	¼ cup chopped onion
	⅓ cup butter, melted
1 tsp. salt	2 whole eggs
¼ tsp. pepper	¾ cup whole milk
	3 Tbs. shortening
1 Tbs. flour	

In a large bowl, stir together the bread cubes, peanuts, salt, and pepper. In a medium skillet, over medium heat, sauté the celery and onion in the butter until the onion is translucent. Combine with the bread mixture. Beat the eggs and milk together and, working to keep the mixture fluffy, combine with the bread. In a small bowl, cream the shortening and stir the flour into it. Spread the shortening mixture over the bottom and sides of an 8-inch ring mold. Spoon the bread mixture into the mold, packing it enough to remove air pockets. Refrigerate for about an hour, then bake in a preheated oven at 350° F. for 40 minutes.

Irish Stew Marcel
8 to 10 hours

This is my father's recipe for Irish Stew and my favorite version. For chicken bouillon, use College Inn brand if you can find it. Or use granules of Steero, dissolved in 2 cups of hot water. The lamb is blanched in water first, then slow-cooked in the bouillon.

Plain Irish Stew   *(recipe on page 52)*

3 lb. boneless lamb shoulder, cut into 1½-inch cubes	1 medium onion, sliced
2 quarts boiling water	1 tsp. salt
	¼ tsp. pepper
2 cups chicken bouillon	1 bay leaf
	2 Tbs. cold water
½ cup scraped carrots, cut into ½-inch cubes	2 Tbs. cornstarch
	1 tsp. strained lemon juice
½ cup scraped turnips, cut into ½-inch cubes	

To Cook: Place the lamb cubes in a kettle with the boiling water and simmer for 15 minutes. Discard the water. Place the bouillon, carrots, turnips, onion, salt, pepper, and bay leaf in the slow cooker and add the blanched lamb. Cover and cook on Low for 8 to 10 hours.

Before Serving: Measure out ½ cup cooking liquid and let cool. Mix the cornstarch with the cold water and combine this with the cooled cooking liquid. Add the lemon juice to this mixture and pour back into the slow cooker. Turn the heat to High and cook the sauce for 10 to 15 minutes — uncovered if the sauce is very thin, covered if thick.
Makes 8 to 10 servings.

Plain Irish Stew
8 to 10 hours

An alternate known to all of us is cooked in the same fashion as Irish Stew Marcel, but the only vegetables are 8 whole small potatoes and 2 celery stalks cut into 1-inch pieces. To make the stew more festive, it is topped with a whole pimiento at the end, while the sauce thickens.

Navarin Printanier
8 to 10 hours

This famous French dish is at its best when the vegetables are spring's early crops. Even in spring, fresh peas can be hard to find, so I usually plan to use frozen.

4 Tbs. butter	1 cup beef bouillon
4 small onions, peeled and sliced	or 1 cup water with 1 beef bouillon cube
4 lb. boneless lamb shoulder or breast, cut into 2-inch cubes	1 tsp. salt
	¼ tsp. pepper
	2 sprigs fresh or ⅛ tsp. dried rosemary
2 lb. small new potatoes, scraped	1 clove garlic, peeled
8 baby carrots, scraped	1 bay leaf
8 baby turnips, peeled	1 package (10 oz.) frozen green peas
3 Tbs. all-purpose flour	

To Cook: In a large skillet over medium heat, melt the butter and sauté the onions until golden. Add the lamb pieces and sauté until golden brown all over. Place the lamb, potatoes, carrots, and turnips in the cooker. Add the flour to the skillet and stir until it turns light brown. Beat in the beef bouillon and stir continuously until the sauce becomes smooth. Turn the sauce into the slow cooker, along with the salt, pepper, rosemary, garlic, and bay leaf. Cover and cook on Low for 8 to 10 hours, or until the meat is completely tender.

Before Serving: About 10 minutes before you are ready to serve, add to the cooker the frozen peas, turn the heat to High, and cook until the peas are tender, about 10 minutes. If the sauce seems thin when you are ready to add the peas, cook the peas with the slow cooker uncovered; if the sauce seems thicker than a cream soup, cover for these last moments of cooking.
Makes 10 to 12 servings.

Other Meats

The slow cooker is a good way to do a number of not-so-common meats you'll find from time to time on the market. Beef heart is delicious, but it's one of the foods that comes out tops only when it is slow-cooked. Tongue benefits from slow cooking in a flavorful broth and so does corned beef. Glance at the recipes in this section and they'll give you ideas and basic guidelines for cooking market offerings you may have considered hard to handle and less than intriguing.

Stuffed Beef Heart
8 to 10 hours

Beef heart is a rich, dark meat with an excellent flavor — and the slow cooker cooks it to perfection.

1 beef heart (3 to 5 lb.)	⅛ tsp. pepper
	1 cup water
¼ cup butter	2 tsp. salt
¼ cup minced onion	½ tsp. pepper
¾ cup lightly packed bread cubes or crumbs	1 tsp. marjoram
	½ tsp. dried thyme
	2 tsp. strained lemon juice
½ tsp. salt	
½ tsp. poultry seasoning	
1 tsp. celery seed	
3 tsp. minced fresh parsley or 1½ tsp. dried parsley flakes	

To Cook: Remove the fat, the veins, and the arteries from the beef heart and wash well. Melt the butter in a medium skillet over medium heat and sauté the onion and bread cubes in it with the ½ teaspoon salt, poultry seasoning, celery seed, parsley, and the ⅛ teaspoon pepper for 5 or 6 minutes. Remove the stuffing to a bowl. In the same skillet, sauté the beef heart on all sides. Remove the heart from the skillet and stuff with the bread mixture. Pour the water into the skillet and scrape up the pan juices. Place the heart, the sauce in the skillet, and all the remaining ingredients except the lemon juice in the slow cooker. Cover and cook on Low for 8 to 10 hours, or until tender.

Before Serving: Remove the heart to a warm serving dish. Turn the cooking liquids into a small skillet, add the lemon juice, and simmer until reduced and slightly thickened.
Makes 4 to 8 servings.

Braised Stuffed Calves' Hearts
6 to 8 hours

These are smaller than beef hearts and are cooked much the same way. Clean and stuff as described for Stuffed Beef Heart (page 52). You will need about 3 calves' hearts to serve 4 to 6 people. Cook the calves' hearts in tomato juice instead of water and cook on Low for 6 to 8 hours, or until tender.

Slow-Cooked Smoked Tongue
8 to 12 hours

Smoked tongue, if you can get one of a size to fit into your slow cooker, is great cooked following the recipe for Slow-Cooked Daisy Ham Roll (page 44). Serve it with prepared mustard or horseradish sauce and with plain boiled potatoes with butter.

Slow-Cooked Polish Sausage
8 to 12 hours

Polish sausage is great done in a slow cooker. Follow the recipe for Slow-Cooked Daisy Ham Roll (page 44) and serve with heated sauerkraut, and with potatoes and carrots boiled together. Offer butter with the potatoes.

Slow-Cooked Corned Beef
8 to 12 hours

Corned beef, cooked ever so slowly in a crockery cooker, is wonderful with rye bread and mustard. A treat as do-your-own sandwiches for a crowd. Or it is wonderful served with fresh green cabbage as a vegetable. Follow the recipe for Slow-Cooked Daisy Ham Roll (page 44).

Beer is the best drink to serve with it.

Onion Soup with Cheese Croutons *The recipe appears on page 58.*

Part III
Soups for Supper — and Luncheon, Too

The slow-cooking pot has not only given us back time we used to spend to make from-scratch foods for the family, it has also given us back one of the nicest and easiest suppers in the world — a hearty soup. Nothing makes as good a soup as a slow cooker.

I've had a romance with soups for years. For one thing, soup is one way I use treasured leftovers. For another, treasured leftovers work wonders for soups.

Using a slow-cooking pot, you can make soups two ways. You can begin soups the night before and have them ready the following day for dinner. Vichyssoise to be served chilled is an example. Let it cook all night. In the morning set it to chill in the refrigerator, and it will be ready to garnish with chives for a cool, delicious dinner that night.

Or you can toss everything into a pot in the morning and have the soup ready to eat the minute you — or anyone — walks in the door.

I use my slow pot to deal with soups yet another way. I start some of the soups that require long cooking the night before and let them simmer through the morning so that the children can help themselves to hot soup when they come home to eat their luncheon sandwiches.

6
Soups That Begin with Leftovers

Among the things usually discarded in the kitchen that can be used for soups are bones of all sorts.

Roasted or baked (but not charcoal-broiled) bones of various beef cuts bring extra flavor to soup. So do bits of gravies saved from the drippings of beef and other roasts. I save bones in the freezer. They stay fresh for several months. When I have enough, I make beef and other bouillons.

Beef bouillon is the same thing as beef stock — that magic ingredient gourmet recipes call for. In the old days beef stock was made from collected beef bones and other scraps. In modern kitchens not equipped with slow pots, making stock has its drawbacks. It uses a lot of gas or electricity. To keep water simmering for hours fills the kitchen with steam and heat. But in the slow cooker, which lets no steam escape whatsoever, stock or bouillon can simmer all day, or all night for that matter, without filling the room with moisture — and for pennies, much less than the cost of buying canned bouillon.

In the slow cooker stock can cook literally all day. Or if you need it in the morning, it can simmer all night and be ready in the morning. Since no water escapes, the pot never goes dry.

Not only beef bones but the bones from leg of lamb roast and other bone-in lamb cuts can be used to make soups, and so can veal. Veal bones can be used interchangeably with chicken bones. In soup recipes veal bones give a flavor particularly their own, but the flavor is so delicate that it blends well into any recipe that calls for chicken stock or bouillon.

Though I save beef, veal, lamb, and ham bones (for pea and lentil soup), there's no need to save chicken bones for soup or bouillon or stock. The tips of chicken wings, the necks, and the backs cooked in a slow pot make excellent chicken stock. These are packaged separately in the plastic containers that hold cut-up whole chicken and can simply be popped into the freezer.

Saving Other Discards to Make Soup

There are lots of other kitchen discards useful for making soup. Celery leaves, carrot peels, the cooking water from fresh vegetables, and gravies (as mentioned above) are some discards that make good stocks and soups. With

Stock from Leftovers *Stock made from leftovers can be stored in 1-cup lots in the freezer, for later use with casserole and stew recipes. Nothing improves the flavor of a dish as does a sauce made with stock instead of water. Stock is one of the things our grandmothers made much of, and the slow-cook pot makes its use possible once more at only pennies in electricity and ingredients.*

Using Discards *Tough outer leaves of cabbage, celery leaves and ends, carrot ends and peelings, parsley stems, chuck of beef bones and chicken back shown here are fine ingredients for use in stocks and soups made in a slow-cook pot.*

this in mind, if you think a little about what goes into the garbage can, you'll realize there are other odds and ends the slow-pot soups can salvage. Putting discards into soups gives one a feeling of great virtue — and gives the soups a great deal of flavor.

The soups in this group are all begun with leftovers. In Chapter 6 you'll find a few hearty soups that can be made starting with saved-up leftovers instead of purchased ingredients.

Dutch Soup with Bread
8 to 10 hours

This uses up stale bread and all sorts of leftovers. I make this starting with bones from steak and beef roasts that I save in the freezer. A half-dozen T-bones (not from steaks that have been roasted over charcoal, please!) or the bones from a medium rib roast will do.

Beef bones (as noted above)	¼ tsp. pepper
1 bay leaf	½ cup finely chopped onions
½ tsp. thyme	3 tsp. butter
1 medium onion, peeled and stuck with 4 whole cloves	6 slices dried-out whole wheat bread
1 tsp. dried parsley	½ cup canned beets, shredded
2 tsp. Steero beef bouillon granules or 2 beef bouillon cubes	½ tsp. caraway seeds
3½ cups water	2 cups shredded fresh green cabbage
2 tsp. salt	1 cup whole milk

To Cook: Place the beef bones, bay leaf, thyme, onion stuck with cloves, parsley, bouillon granules or cubes, water, salt, and pepper in the slow cooker, cover, and cook on Low for 8 to 10 hours.

Before Serving: Discard the bones. In a large skillet, over medium heat, sauté the onions in the butter until golden brown. Add the bread slices, 2 cups of the beef stock from the slow cooker, the beets, and the caraway seeds. Simmer 15 minutes. Add the cabbage and simmer 10 minutes. Stir in the milk and heat through. (Save remaining beef stock for future use.) Makes 6 to 8 servings.

Imperial Carrot Soup

Imperial Carrot Soup
6 to 8 hours

A hearty chicken soup with — surprise — a carrot flavor. It is made with chicken discards — wing tips, necks, backs — you can save up in the freezer.

8 to 10 wing tips, 4 to 6 necks, and 2 to 3 backs of chicken	2 tsp. salt ¼ tsp. pepper 3 whole cloves
1 medium onion, peeled and chopped	2 Tbs. butter 3 cups thinly sliced carrots
2½ cups water	¼ tsp. coriander (optional)
2 tsp. Steero chicken bouillon granules or 2 chicken bouillon cubes	1 cup whole milk or half-and-half
1 bay leaf	1 tsp. freeze-dried or fresh chives
½ tsp. thyme	

To Cook: Place the chicken parts in the slow cooker, along with the onion, water, chicken bouillon granules or cubes, bay leaf, thyme, salt, pepper, and cloves. Cover and cook on Low for 6 to 8 hours.

Before Serving: Discard the chicken parts, bay leaf, and cloves. In a large skillet, over low heat, melt the butter and sauté the carrot slices. Scoop a little chicken stock from the pot into the skillet, mix, add the coriander if desired, and turn the stock back into the pot with the carrots. Turn the slow cooker to High and cook for about 10 minutes, or until the carrots are very tender. Add the milk to the pot. Reserve a few slices of carrot. Using a blender on Low, blend the remaining carrots and the soup, 2 cups at a time. Turn into a tureen and garnish with reserved carrot slices and chives. Makes 4 to 6 servings.

Onion Soup with Cheese Croutons
8 to 10 hours

Make onion soup with saved-up chicken parts and beef bones.

8 to 10 wing tips, 4 to 6 necks, and 2 to 3 backs of chicken	2 tsp. salt ¼ tsp. pepper 3 whole cloves
2½ cups water	Bones from beef rib roast and steaks
1 medium onion, peeled and chopped	4 cups thinly sliced onions
2 tsp. Steero chicken bouillon granules or 2 chicken bouillon cubes	¼ cup butter 2 Tbs. all-purpose flour
1 bay leaf	3½ cups water
½ tsp. thyme	Puffy Cheese Croutons (see below)

To Cook: Place the chicken and the next 9 ingredients in the slow cooker, cover, and cook on Low for 8 to 10 hours.

Before Serving: Discard the meat bones. In a large skillet, over medium-low heat, sauté the onion slices in the butter but do not brown them. Lower the heat. Stir in the flour to make a smooth mixture. Add 2 cups of the broth from the cooker all at once and beat quickly to smooth the roux. Turn the sauce in the skillet into the slow cooker, add 3½ cups water, cover, and cook on High for about 10 minutes. Serve the soup topped with Puffy Cheese Croutons. Makes 4 to 6 servings.

Puffy Cheese Croutons

¼ cup butter	2 egg whites
1 Tbs. milk	French bread cut into
1 cup (¼ lb.) shredded	bite-size pieces
aged Cheddar cheese	

Turn the oven to 400° F. Melt butter in the top section of a double boiler over hot, but not boiling, water or in a small saucepan over very low heat. Add milk; stir in cheese, stirring constantly until the cheese is melted. Remove from the heat. Beat the egg whites until stiff but not dry. Gently fold beaten egg whites into the cheese mixture. Dip bread cubes into the egg-cheese mixture and place on ungreased baking sheet. Bake in preheated oven 10 to 15 minutes or until slightly browned. Remove immediately.

Onion Soup Supreme
6 to 8 hours

Another onion soup made good by using chicken parts you often discard.

8 to 10 wing tips, 4 to	1 tsp. thyme
6 necks, and 2 to	2 tsp. salt
3 backs of chicken	¼ tsp. pepper
1 medium onion,	2 cups thinly sliced
peeled and	onions
chopped	2 Tbs. butter
2½ cups water	3 Tbs. all-purpose
2 tsp. Steero chicken	flour
bouillon granules	½ tsp. dry mustard
or 2 chicken	3 cups whole milk
bouillon cubes	½ tsp. ground
1 bay leaf	coriander
¼ tsp. paprika	

To Cook: Place the chicken parts in the slow cooker, along with the onion, water, chicken bouillon granules or cubes, bay leaf, thyme, salt, and pepper. Cover and cook on Low for 6 to 8 hours.

Before Serving: Discard the chicken parts. In a medium kettle, over medium-low heat, sauté the onions in the butter until the onion is golden. Blend in the flour and the dry mustard and at once add a cup of hot chicken stock from the pot. Stir to smooth the mixture, then add the milk and coriander. Stir this into the stock in the slow cooker, turn the heat to High for a minute or two, then pour into a tureen. Garnish with paprika.
Makes 4 to 6 servings.

Parsley Soup Peasant Style
10 to 12 hours

This is a family favorite. The broken chunks of stale French bread are well buttered before we put them into the soup plates and they soften as they absorb the bouillon, until they are just right to eat — and deliciously filled with broth.

2½ tsp. salt	½ tsp. thyme
1 lb. stew beef, cut	2 medium cloves
into 1-inch cubes	garlic, peeled
8 cups water	¼ cup finely minced
2 quarts beef bones	parsley
with meat bits	4 to 8 chunks really
on them	stale French
2 medium carrots,	bread, well but-
scraped	tered on each side
2 medium onions,	¼ cup dry red wine
peeled and stuck	(optional)
with 6 whole	
cloves	
2 sprigs fresh	
parsley or 1 tsp.	
dried parsley	

To Cook: In a large skillet, over medium-high heat, sprinkle the salt and brown the beef on all sides. Brown it really well. Pour a cupful of the water into the skillet, scrape up the pan juices, and turn the whole thing into the slow cooker. Add all the other ingredients in the recipe, except wine, bread, and parsley, cover, and cook on Low for 10 to 12 hours. Strain.

Before Serving: Mix the wine into the hot bouillon and turn the heat to High and simmer, uncovered, for 3 to 4 minutes. Place the bread chunks in the serving bowls, divide the minced parsley among the bowls, pour the soup over the top, and serve at once.
Makes 4 to 6 servings.

Beef Bouillon or Stock
10 to 12 hours

This is an excellent basic bouillon from which you can make all sorts of delicious soups and stews and casseroles. Add beef bouillon to the pan in which beef has baked or roasted just before it finishes cooking, scrape up the pan juices, and you'll have a delicious gravy. I save beef bones with bits of meat on them in the freezer to make this.

2½ tsp. salt	½ tsp. thyme
1 lb. stew beef, cut into 1-inch cubes	2 medium cloves garlic, peeled
8 cups water	2 medium carrots, scraped
2 quarts beef bones with meat bits on them	2 medium onions, peeled and stuck with 6 whole cloves
2 sprigs fresh parsley, or 1 tsp. dried parsley	

To Cook: In a large skillet, over medium-high heat, sprinkle the salt and brown the beef on all sides. Brown it really well. Pour a cupful of the water into the skillet, scrape up the pan juices, and turn the whole thing into the slow cooker. Add all the other ingredients in the recipe, cover, and cook on Low for 10 to 12 hours. Strain.
Makes about 8½ cups.

Split-Pea Soup
8 to 10 hours

This is another favorite. I make it with a leftover ham bone, and the slow pot cooks it to perfection. You can sauté the onions first in butter, but the easiest, hurry-up way is the one described below.

2 Tbs. butter	1 cup finely minced celery
1 cup minced onion	
8 cups water	1 cup diced carrots
2 cups (1 lb.) green split peas, washed	⅛ tsp. savory
	⅛ tsp. dried marjoram
4 whole cloves	
1 bay leaf	1 Tbs. salt
1 ham bone	¼ tsp. pepper

To Cook: Place all the ingredients in the slow cooker, cover, and cook on Low for 8 to 10 hours.
Before Serving: I like this soup to be really thick, and after the first long-cook period, I generally simmer it down to a consistency that almost lets you stand a matchstick in it. If you want to try it that way, uncover the soup, turn the heat to High, and simmer, stirring occasionally, until the desired consistency is reached. The peas may stick to the bottom during this second cooking period, so do not forget to stir occasionally. If you want the finished soup thinner instead of thicker, thin it with milk — it's delicious. Remove the ham bone and bay leaf before serving and dice any meat from the bone and return it to the soup.
Makes 6 to 8 servings.

Lentil Soup with a Ham Bone
8 to 10 hours

I usually make this soup with a ham bone but both lentil and pea soup are almost as good made instead with the broth left over from the cooking of a Slow-Cooked Daisy Ham Roll (page 44). So if you don't have a ham bone and want lentil or pea soup, plan to make the Slow-Cooked Daisy Ham Roll the day before you make the soup.

2 Tbs. butter	1 cup finely minced celery
1 cup minced onion	
8 cups water	1 cup diced carrots
2 cups (1 lb.) lentils, washed	⅛ tsp. savory
	⅔ tsp. dried marjoram
4 whole cloves	
1 bay leaf	1 Tbs. salt
1 ham bone	¼ tsp. pepper

To Cook: Place all the ingredients in the slow cooker, cover, turn the heat to Low, and cook for 8 to 10 hours.
Before Serving: Remove the ham bone and the bay leaf. Dice the meat and fat from the bone and return to the soup.
Makes 6 to 8 servings.

7
Soups That Make
One-Dish Dinners

The soups grouped here are hearty, so hearty that they make meals all by themselves. Most begin with simple cuts of meat that require lots of cooking of the type the slow pot does superbly. The recipe for Leek Soup is a classic that lends itself to all sorts of variations. Others, like Bouillabaisse, invite your own creativity. In France it's made with the day's catch of fish and shellfish. Bait a hook and send the family fishing! Use approximations of the fish ingredients described in the recipe here.

Beef Gumbo Soup, Baked Bean Soup, and Beef and Cabbage Soup are typical of soups that make a satisfying meal when served with bread products. Sweet and hot rolls and biscuits dripping with melted butter (this is not a diet book) make soup meals memorable occasions and as easy on the cook as they are on the budget.

And — you don't need meat to make a soup fit for a king (or queen). You can make very satisfying meal-in-one soups with just vegetables and grains. A big bowl of Corn Chowder (with or without the luxury of a few oysters) makes a meal. If the diners have room to spare, plan a pastry dessert. Or, follow the chowder with a green salad and fresh fruit. The vegetable soup recipe on page 66 is my mother's. As a child, it was one of my favorite dishes, so good I always wanted two servings, and never had room enough to eat anything else except a piece of fruit. Francesca Morris's recipe for Scotch Broth is another family favorite. Francesca makes it when she has a bone left over from a roast leg of lamb. There's little meat on the bone, but the vegetables and barley (a wholesome and nutritious grain) make the soup as filling as a three-course meal.

But meals composed mainly, or only, of soup aren't always and only budget trimmers: Vichyssoise is one of the most delightful — and sophisticated — dishes you can serve for lunch, and Egg Drop Soup, a Chinese favorite, makes a conversation piece. Clam Chowder is another meal-in-one soup everyone loves and gourmets treasure.

Try them the slow-cook way. It really makes it all much easier.

Bouillabaisse
5 to 8 hours

The seafood soup/stew called Bouillabaisse comes from the southern shores of France, where it is the custom to add all the day's catch, whatever it is, to the simmering kettle. This formalized version can include cod, flounder, haddock, red snapper, sea bass, or perch. The fish must be very fresh. If you catch it yourself, fillet it and save the head and the bones. Shellfish suited to Bouillabaisse are crab, lobster, lobster or crayfish tails, and scallops.

4 lb. fish fillets (see above)	2 cloves garlic, peeled
2 lb. shellfish	6 cups water
16 to 24 mussels or steamer clams, cleaned	Fish trimmings (see above)
½ cup olive oil	1 medium carrot, peeled and halved
½ cup chopped leeks or onions	1 bay leaf
2 large tomatoes, peeled and seeded, or 1 cup canned whole tomatoes, drained and cut up	½ Tbs. salt
	⅛ tsp. pepper
	⅛ tsp. ground saffron
	6 to 8 slices stale French bread

To Cook: Cut the large fish fillets on a slant into slices about 2 inches wide. If you are using lobster, split the lobster; if crab, lift the tail flap of the crab. Refrigerate the fish and shellfish. In a large skillet, over medium heat, heat the oil and sauté the leeks or onions until translucent, about 5 minutes. Swish the tomatoes around in the skillet and turn the skillet contents into the slow cooker. Add the garlic, water, fish trimmings, carrot, bay leaf, salt, pepper, and saffron. Cover and cook on Low for 5 to 8 hours.

Before Serving: Remove the fish trimmings from the slow pot. Turn the heat to Medium High or, if your cooker has no in-between places, to High. Add the shellfish to the stock, cover, allow the soup to return to a boil, and simmer for 10 minutes. Add firm-fleshed fillets (snapper, bass, perch) and cover and simmer for 5 minutes. Add the soft-fleshed fish (cod, flounder, haddock) and the mussels, scallops, or clams. When the soup returns to a boil, simmer for 5 minutes more. To serve the Bouillabaisse, place a slice of stale French bread into each bowl and include a portion of each type of shellfish and fish in each serving.
Makes 8 to 10 generous servings.

Leek Soup
5 to 7 hours

This is a basic recipe from which all sorts of variations can be made. The most famous is the recipe following this one, called Vichyssoise. Add milk to Leek Soup, and the flavor changes. Dress it with a dab of curry, and the flavor changes. Mince half a cup of parsley very finely and sprinkle it over the hot soup after serving, and you have a whole new soup affair going.

4 large or 6 small leeks	1 quart water
2 Tbs. butter	3 cups potatoes, peeled and diced
1 small onion, peeled and chopped	½ tsp. salt
	1 Tbs. butter

To Cook: Washing the leeks is important. Any sand left inside will make the soup a lot less fun to eat, especially when you get to the bottom of the pot. Cut the leeks in half and remove yellowed or wilted outer leaves. Fill the sink with water and wash each leek leaf until absolutely clean. Rinse under cold running water. In a medium skillet, over medium heat, melt the butter and sauté the onion until translucent. Don't let it brown. Pour a little of the water into the skillet and turn the skillet contents into the slow pot. Place all the remaining ingredients and the leeks in the pot, except the final tablespoon of butter. Cover and cook on Low for 5 to 7 hours.

Before Serving: Mash the ingredients in the soup together to make a smooth cream. Add a dab of butter to each serving. If you'd like the soup thinner, add a little milk.
Makes 4 to 6 servings.

Vichyssoise
5 to 7 hours

This is the fancy version of Leek Soup. It's lovely hot, and divine cold. To serve it cold, let it cook all night and chill, covered, all day in the refrigerator; then add the chives and serve.

Vichyssoise

Chicken Bouillon
10 to 12 hours

This is the basic recipe my family uses for making chicken bouillon. Serve the chicken, cut from the bones if you like, in a soup plate filled with broth. Add croutons to dress it up for special occasions. Save any broth left over and freeze it in one-cup lots; any casserole or stew made with a bouillon will turn out a great deal better than one made with plain water. To make economy chicken bouillon or stock, use saved-up wing tips, necks, and backs instead of a chicken or chicken pieces.

2½ lb. chicken, cut up	6 black peppercorns
1 small onion, peeled	2 sprigs fresh parsley or 1 tsp. dried parsley
1 medium carrot, scraped	1 bay leaf
1 medium parsnip, peeled	½ tsp. thyme
2 medium cloves garlic, peeled	2 tsp. salt
	8 cups water

To Cook: Place all the ingredients in the slow cooker, cover, and cook on Low for 10 to 12 hours. If the flavor seems a little pale, add more salt and pepper at the end. Strain. Makes 8 to 8½ cups.

5 large or 8 small leeks
2 Tbs. butter
1 very small onion, peeled and minced
1 quart chicken bouillon or 4 cups water with Steero chicken bouillon granules

3 cups diced potatoes
1 Tbs. salt
1 cup heavy cream
2 Tbs. chopped chives

To Cook: Wash the leeks carefully. Cut them in half and remove spoiled or wilted outer leaves and the green portions of the other leaves. Wash leaves one at a time in a sinkful of cold water. When all dirt is gone, rinse under cold water once more. In a medium skillet, over medium heat, melt the butter and sauté the onion until golden and translucent. Don't let the onion brown at all. Pour a little of the chicken bouillon into the skillet and turn the skillet contents into the slow pot. Add the potatoes, salt, and leeks, cover, and cook on Low for 5 to 7 hours.

Before Serving: In a blender on Low, blend the soup 2 cups at a time. Taste and add salt if needed. Combine with cream and serve hot, garnished with chopped chives. Or chill for several hours, then combine with heavy cream and garnish each serving with chives. Makes 4 to 6 servings.

Chicken Bouillon Chinese Style
10 to 12 hours

2½ lb. chicken, cut up	2 sprigs fresh parsley or 1 tsp. dried parsley
1 small onion, peeled	1 bay leaf
1 medium carrot, scraped	1 tsp. soy sauce
2 white radishes, scraped	2 slices fresh ginger, ½ inch thick, or 1 tsp. ground ginger
2 medium cloves garlic, peeled	2 tsp. salt
6 black peppercorns	8 cups water

To Cook: Place all the ingredients in the slow cooker, cover, and cook on Low for 10 to 12 hours. If the flavor seems a little pale, add more salt and pepper at the end. Strain. Makes 8 to 8½ cups.

Beef Gumbo Soup

Beef Gumbo Soup
6 to 8 hours

This is a hearty meat and vegetable soup that makes a complete meal. Serve a good portion of meat in each soup plate.

2 to 3 lb. cross-cut beef shanks, cut 2 inches thick	½ cup diced celery
1 Tbs. butter	1 can (16 oz.) whole tomatoes
1 quart water	1 package (10 oz.) frozen lima beans
1 Tbs. salt	1 package (9 oz.) frozen cut green beans
¼ tsp. pepper	
1 bay leaf	1 can (16 oz.) whole kernel corn
1 medium onion, peeled and quartered	
6 medium carrots, peeled and diced	¼ head green cabbage, sliced fine
1 cup peeled, diced potato	1 can (16 oz.) okra, drained

To Cook: In a large skillet, over medium-high heat, brown the shanks in the butter. Place the shanks in the slow-cook pot with the water, salt, pepper, bay leaf, onion, carrots, potato, celery, and tomatoes. Cover and cook on Low for 6 to 8 hours.

Before Serving: Turn the heat to High and add the lima beans, green beans, corn, and cabbage. Simmer uncovered for 20 to 30 minutes. Add the okra and heat thoroughly.
Makes 6 to 8 servings.

Beef and Cabbage Soup
6 to 8 hours

A hearty soup; serve with bread to make a complete meal.

Beef and Cabbage Soup

1½ lb. top round or sirloin tip, cut into 2-inch cubes	1 large clove garlic, peeled and minced
2 Tbs. vegetable oil	2 tsp. salt
4 cups water	½ tsp. pepper
1 Tbs. soy sauce	½ tsp. dry mustard
4 cups shredded cabbage	2 large potatoes, peeled and diced
1 cup chopped onion	2 large sweet potatoes, peeled and diced
¼ lb. bacon, minced	2 Tbs. ketchup or chili sauce

To Cook: In a medium skillet, over medium heat, sauté the beef cubes in the oil until dark brown on all sides. Add the water, the soy sauce, 3 cups of the cabbage, the onion, bacon, garlic, salt, pepper, mustard, potatoes (both kinds), and the ketchup. Cover and cook on Low for 6 to 8 hours.

Before Serving: Uncover, turn the heat to High, add the remaining cabbage, simmer until tender — about 15 minutes — and then serve.
Makes 6 to 8 servings.

Curry Soup

Curry Soup
8 to 10 hours

This is especially good if you have a really good curry powder to make it with.

1 lb. boneless lamb or veal cut into 2-inch cubes	6 cups water
2 Tbs. oil	6 tsp. Steero chicken bouillon granules or 6 chicken bouillon cubes
¼ cup butter	
1 cup thinly sliced onion	1 apple, peeled, cored, and diced
½ cup thinly sliced carrot	1 bay leaf
½ cup thinly sliced white turnip	⅛ tsp. thyme
	1 cup converted rice
2 tsp. curry powder	1 tsp. strained lemon juice

To Cook: In a large skillet, over medium heat, sauté the lamb or veal in the oil until lightly browned on all sides. Remove to the slow cooker. Add the onion, carrot, turnip, and curry powder to the skillet. Sauté in butter for 3 or 4 minutes. Pour the water and chicken bouillon granules or cubes into the skillet, scraping up the pan juices, and turn into the cooker. Add the apple, bay leaf, thyme, and rice. Cover and cook on Low for 8 to 10 hours.

Before Serving: Stir the lemon juice into the soup and serve.

Makes 8 to 10 servings.

Beans and Ham Soup
18 to 20 hours

This soup combines beans with a small ham shank and makes a complete and very hearty meal for a crowd. Start this the night before. The beans must be soaked overnight before cooking.

1 lb. dried white beans, soaked	1 cup shredded carrots
1 small smoked ham shank	¼ cup minced parsley
8 cups water	2 cloves garlic, peeled and minced
2 cups chopped onion	2 to 3 tsp. salt
1 cup chopped celery	1 tsp. pepper

To Cook: The night before, measure the beans and place them in the slow cooker. Measure three times as much water as beans and add to the pot. Cover and cook on Low overnight. In the morning, drain away any water that remains. Add the remaining ingredients to the cooker, cover, and cook on Low for 6 to 8 hours more.

Beans and Ham Soup

Before Serving: Remove the ham to a cutting board. Remove the bone and dice the meat. While you are doing this, simmer the soup in the cooker on High if it seems thin. Return the diced meat to the soup.

Makes 8 to 10 servings.

Chicken Soup with Rice
10 to 12 hours

2½ lb. chicken, cut up	2 medium cloves
1 small onion, peeled and chopped	garlic, peeled
	6 black peppercorns
1 medium carrot, scraped and cut into 1-inch pieces	2 sprigs fresh parsley or 1 tsp. dried parsley
	1 bay leaf
1 medium parsnip, peeled and cut into 1-inch pieces	½ tsp. thyme
	1 cup raw rice
	2 tsp. salt
8 cups water	

To Cook: Place all the ingredients in the slow cooker, cover, and cook on Low for 10 to 12 hours. Remove the chicken pieces from the soup after cooking, skin and bone the meat, cut into small cubes, and return to the soup. If the flavor seems a little pale, add more salt and pepper at the end.
Makes 8½ to 9 cups.

Hearty Cream of Chicken Soup
10 to 12 hours

This is a variation of chicken bouillon. Kids love it.

2½ lb. chicken, cut up	6 black peppercorns
1 small onion, peeled	2 sprigs fresh parsley or 1 tsp. dried parsley
1 medium carrot, scraped and cut into 1-inch pieces	1 bay leaf
	½ tsp. thyme
1 medium parsnip, peeled and cut into 1-inch pieces	1 cup raw rice
	2 tsp. salt
	8 cups water
2 medium cloves garlic, peeled	3 Tbs. all-purpose flour

To Cook: Place all the ingredients except the flour in the slow cooker, cover, and cook on Low for 10 to 12 hours.
Before Serving: Remove the chicken parts from the soup and allow to cool. Then skin and bone the meat, cut into small cubes, and set aside. Skim 2 tablespoons of chicken fat from the soup and place it in a medium skillet over medium-low heat. Stir in the flour, then beat in all at once a cup or so of chicken bouillon. Work quickly to keep the sauce smooth. Allow it to simmer for 5 or 6 minutes on the stove top, then turn it back into the slow cooker. Return the cubed chicken to the soup, raise the heat to High and simmer for 2 or 3 minutes before serving.
Makes 6 to 8 servings.

Egg Drop Soup

This is a favorite soup for those who love Chinese food, and since its basis is Chicken Bouillon Chinese Style, I include it here. It's light — not a soup that makes a complete supper. Let the slow cooker make the basic chicken bouillon while you are away and finish the soup just before serving dinner.

4 to 5 cups Chicken Bouillon Chinese Style (page 63)	½ tsp. salt
	2 whole eggs
	1 scallion, minced
1 Tbs. cornstarch	1 tsp. Chinese parsley, minced (optional, but don't use regular parsley)
½ tsp. soy sauce	
3 Tbs. Chicken Bouillon Chinese Style, cold	

To Cook: Heat the chicken bouillon to a simmer in a large kettle over medium heat. Mix the cornstarch and the soy sauce in a small container and add 3 tablespoons cold chicken bouillon. Add the salt, stir thoroughly, and pour the mixture into the soup. Stir until the soup has thickened and cleared (it will cloud when you add the cornstarch). Break the eggs into a bowl, mix just a little, and in a thin stream pour the eggs slowly — *slowly* — into the soup. Remove the soup from the heat and stir it once. Divide the scallion and the parsley among the soup plates and ladle the soup over the top.
Makes 4 to 6 servings.

Mother's Vegetable Soup
6 to 8 hours

One of my favorite memories is eating this soup for a late, light supper, with plain bread and butter.

1 large onion, peeled and chopped	3 large potatoes, peeled and diced
1 Tbs. butter	2 large sprigs fresh parsley, minced
5 cups water	
4 carrots, peeled and diced	1 cup diced celery
½ medium yellow turnip, peeled and diced	2 tsp. salt
	¼ tsp. pepper

To Cook: In a medium skillet, over medium heat, sauté the onions in the butter until translucent, about 4 or 5 minutes. Pour a little of the water into the skillet and scrape the water and onions into the slow cooker. Add all the ingredients to the slow cooker, cover, and cook on Low for 6 to 8 hours.
Makes 4 to 6 servings.

Francesca Morris's Recipe for Scotch Broth
6 to 8 hours

When Francesca has a leftover lamb bone, she makes this soup with it. You'll have to break the bone to fit it into the slow cooker. If you want to start from scratch, use lamb shoulder.

3 lb. lamb shoulder, bone in, or a leftover lamb bone	1 large onion, peeled and diced
	1½ tsp. salt
	⅛ tsp. pepper
6 cups cold water	1 cup barley, raw
1 bay leaf	2 Tbs. butter
1 cup diced carrots	2 Tbs. flour
1 cup diced celery	2 Tbs. finely chopped parsley
1 cup leeks, washed and sliced small	

To Cook: Cut the meat into 2-inch cubes and place, with the bone, in the slow cooker. Place the remaining ingredients except the butter, flour, and parsley in the slow cooker. Cover and cook on Low for 6 to 8 hours.
Before Serving: In a small saucepan, over low heat, melt the butter and stir the flour into it. Pour one cup of hot soup from the slow cooker into the flour and stir quickly to make a smooth sauce. Mix this back into the soup. Cook the soup, uncovered, at High for about 5

minutes, stirring occasionally. Remove the bones, garnish with parsley, and serve.
Makes 10 to 12 servings.

Corn Chowder

Corn Chowder
6 to 8 hours

This is one of my personal favorites, but it isn't really right unless you make it with salt pork. Bacon, which a lot of cooks use as a substitute for salt pork, won't be as good.

⅛ lb. salt pork, cut in ½-inch cubes	2 tsp. salt
	⅛ tsp. pepper
1 large onion, diced	⅛ tsp. paprika
3 cups diced potatoes	⅛ medium green pepper, diced
1½ cups water	2 cups whole milk
1 can (12 oz.) whole corn kernels	½ cup oysters and liquid (optional)

To Cook: In a medium skillet, over medium-high heat, sauté the salt pork until crisp and brown. Remove the bits, drain on a paper towel, and refrigerate. Add the onion, potatoes, water, and corn to the slow cooker, with the salt, pepper, and paprika. Cover and cook on Low for 6 to 8 hours.
Before Serving: Turn the cooker to High and add the green pepper to the soup. Simmer for 5 to 10 minutes, or until the peppers are tender. Add the milk and warm it through. Place the pork bits in the serving bowls and ladle the soup over them.
Makes 6 servings.

Clam Chowder
4 to 5 hours

Quahogs are great big, hard-shell clams; if these aren't available, use small hard-shell clams or steamers.

1 quart of shucked quahog clams or 2 dozen small hard-shell clams, shucked, or soft-shelled steamers
¼ lb. salt pork, diced
1 large onion, peeled and finely minced
4 cups water
3 medium potatoes, peeled and sliced thin
½ tsp. salt
⅛ tsp. pepper
4 cups whole milk
6 large crackers, split
2 Tbs. butter

To Cook: Strain the clams and reserve the clam liquor. Remove the tough neck portion from each clam. Separate the belly, or soft part, from the firm part. Chop the firm parts and put the soft parts in the refrigerator, covered. In a medium skillet, over medium heat, sauté the salt pork until crisp and golden. Drain on paper towels. Sauté the onion until translucent. Add the water and clam liquor to the skillet and scoop the skillet contents into the slow cooker. Add the potatoes, salt, pepper, salt pork bits, and the chopped firm parts of the clams, and cover. Cook on Low for 4 to 5 hours.

Before Serving: Add the milk, cover, and turn the heat to High. When the milk is simmering, turn off the heat, add the soft portions of the clams, cover, and allow to sit for 15 to 20 minutes before serving. Place the crackers in the serving bowls, add a bit of butter to each and ladle the chowder over them.
Makes 6 to 8 servings.

Baked Bean Soup
18 to 20 hours

This is an overnight job. Start the beans the night before and let the soup finish up during

Baked Bean Soup

the day. A nice way to use up leftover ham. The beans *must* be soaked 4 hours before the cooking starts.

1 cup navy beans, soaked
3 cups water
1 cup diced ham
2 Tbs. chopped onions
2 Tbs. bacon drippings or drippings from ham
1 can (16 oz.) whole tomatoes
1 Tbs. brown sugar, tightly packed
2 Tbs. vinegar
1 tsp. salt
2 Tbs. chili sauce or taco sauce

To Cook: The night before, place the soaked beans and the water in the slow cooker and cook on Low until morning. In the morning, sauté the ham and the onions in the bacon drippings in a small skillet. Add them and the tomatoes, sugar, vinegar, and salt to the slow pot. Cover and cook on Low until the beans are tender, another 4 to 6 hours.

Before Serving: Mash the beans a little to thicken the soup, but leave some of them whole to give it body. Flavor with a dash of chili sauce in each soup plate. If the soup seems too thick, thin with a little boiling water before serving. Check for seasoning; it may need salt.
Makes 4 to 6 servings.

Part IV
Vegetables and Side Dishes

8
Casseroles of Vegetable Mélanges

Casseroles that combine vegetables that have lots of moisture are excellent done in a slow cooker. Ratatouille, the southern French classic that combines tomatoes, eggplant, pepper, zucchini, and onions is typical. You can make up your own ratatouille using any combination of these vegetables that your garden offers at the moment. You can adapt your own favorite mélanges as long as the combination includes vegetables that contain a lot of moisture — tomatoes with beans for instance. Tomatoes and onions, flavored with oregano, give an Italian flavor to any dish. Tomatoes and onions and sugar make the mélange taste more American.

Casseroles combining moisture-giving vegetables with dry ingredients of another type work well, too, in the slow cooker. Stuffed Cabbage Rolls is one. You can stuff cabbage leaves with your own favorite mixture and slow-cook them according to the timing of the cabbage roll recipe here.

Root vegetables plain can be cooked as in the Casserole on page 74 or the Turnip and Carrot Pot. Make up your own combination or adapt your own favorite recipe. Use the timing of the recipes here for root vegetables. The color of the vegetables may be less attractive than when they are cooked more quickly, but they will be cooking while you are out playing — and they will taste good.

You can make vegetable puddings (which are rather like soufflés) in a crockery cooker, as long as the cooker is large enough to take the baking casserole the recipe fits. The casserole must sit on a trivet in the cooker and must have a lid. You can improvise a baking unit as described on the following page in the remarks about baking potatoes, if your cooker does not come equipped with a unit. Use the Corn Pudding recipe (page 77) to help adapt your own favorite recipe for vegetable mousse or pudding.

If you study the basic recipes in this chapter for the cooking of fresh vegetables — and in the next chapter for the cooking of grains and beans — you will find it easy to adapt your own favorites to slow crockery cooking.

You can cook fresh vegetables in the slow cooker, but I generally don't. Fresh vegetables really taste best when they are cooked as quickly and as little as possible. The slow cooker doesn't do that, even on High. Fresh vegetables cook quickly, except for the firm root vegetables such as potatoes and carrots and turnips, so they are little enough trouble to cook in regular utensils. To sacrifice flavor by slow cooking them when you aren't saving much time in the process doesn't seem the best use of the cooker or your time.

One fresh vegetable the cooker does well is baked potatoes, and to find them ready to eat when you get home can be helpful. However, they can only be baked inside the type of cooker that takes a baking unit; otherwise, the steady drip of steam from the top of the cooker leaves them soggy. You can improvise a baking unit if your cooker isn't equipped with one by setting the potatoes inside a small ceramic or glass bowl and covering the bowl with a saucer that fits loosely enough to let steam escape from inside into the cooker.

There are some fresh vegetable combinations that are great done in a slow cooker and which can't be done quickly without a lot of trouble. Ratatouille is one of these, and the slow cooker does it to perfection.

Mme. Bertrand's Ratatouille
6 to 8 hours

When I lived in southern France, my landlady taught me to make this as she did, in a crockery saucepan on the back of a wood-burning stove. The crockery cooker is the only dish that gets it just right in a modern kitchen.

⅓ cup olive oil	2 medium zucchini,
3 large cloves garlic, minced	unpeeled, cut into 4-inch pieces
4 large firm tomatoes, cut into 2-inch chunks	3 medium onions, peeled and quartered
1 medium eggplant, peeled and cut into 2-inch cubes	2 tsp. salt
	¼ tsp. pepper
	½ tsp. oregano
2 red or green sweet peppers, seeded and cut into large strips	½ tsp. thyme

To Cook: In a large skillet, heat the oil and sauté the garlic for about 2 minutes. In a large bowl, gently combine the vegetables with the herbs. Turn the garlic and oil into the slow cooker, add the vegetables, cover, and cook on Low for 6 to 8 hours.

Before Serving: If there's a lot of liquid in the ratatouille after everything in it is cooked soft, turn the heat to High and simmer uncovered until the liquid has gone.
Makes 10 to 12 servings.

Tomato Casserole
6 to 8 hours

Tastes like stuffed tomatoes, but the texture is very different.

2 Tbs. butter	3 Tbs. water
1 medium onion, peeled and minced	1 Tbs. soy sauce
	3 Tbs. minced parsley
1 clove garlic, peeled and minced	3 Tbs. butter
½ lb. sausage meat	6 large tomatoes, stemmed and cut into thick slices
1 tsp. salt	
2 tsp. granulated sugar	¾ cup bread crumbs
¾ cup unflavored bread crumbs	Butter

To Cook: In a medium skillet, over medium heat, melt the butter and sauté the onion and garlic until the onion begins to brown. Add the sausage meat, salt, and sugar and sauté for 3 minutes more. Add ¾ cup bread crumbs to the skillet and moisten with water mixed with soy sauce. Mix well and remove from the heat. Sprinkle with parsley. Smear the bottom and sides of the slow cooker with butter. Place ⅓ of the tomato slices on the bottom and add a layer of the bread crumbs and onion mixture. Repeat and end with a layer of tomatoes. Cover and cook on Low for 6 to 8 hours.

Before Serving: Heat the broiler to medium, turn the tomato into an oven-proof baking dish, sprinkle thickly with bread crumbs, and broil long enough to brown the crumbs.
Makes 6 servings.

Green Pepper Casserole
6 to 8 hours

Make this with leftover ground veal or lamb. Or a tag end of raw hamburger works well.

2 Tbs. olive oil
2 medium onions, peeled and chopped
1 cup ground cooked veal or lamb
2 large tomatoes, peeled and chopped
1 clove garlic, peeled and minced
1 tsp. salt
⅛ tsp. pepper
1 bay leaf, crushed
½ tsp. thyme
1 cup raw rice
2 Tbs. butter
8 large green peppers, seeded and sliced into 1-inch strips
1 cup tomato sauce
½ tsp. minced fresh basil or ¼ tsp. dried basil

To Cook: In a large skillet, heat the oil and sauté the onions until golden brown. Mix in the meat and brown it a little, stirring constantly. Stir in the tomatoes, garlic, salt, pepper, bay bits, thyme, and raw rice. Sauté another couple of minutes until the rice begins to look opaque. Smear the butter over the bottom and sides of the slow cooker. Layer the green pepper strips and the tomato mixture in the casserole, ending with peppers. Pour the tomato sauce over all and sprinkle with basil. Cover and cook on Low for 6 to 8 hours.
Makes 8 servings.

Stuffed Cabbage Rolls with Tomato Sauce

Stuffed Cabbage Rolls with Tomato Sauce
6 to 8 hours

A wonderful dish for the family on a cold night. The preparation in advance is a little tedious because you have to make the cabbage rolls, but it can cook all day and is ready whenever you are.

1 medium head of green cabbage
1 lb. (2 cups) chopped, cooked beef, veal, or pork
¼ cup raw rice
1 egg, slightly beaten
1 medium onion, peeled and grated
1 medium carrot, grated
1 tsp. salt
¼ cup malt vinegar
½ cup tightly packed light brown sugar
1 cup canned tomato sauce

To Cook: Drop the cabbage into a large kettle of boiling water and cook for 4 to 8 minutes or until the outer leaves come off easily. Drain and cool. Remove 8 of the large outer leaves. Discard the tough inner core and chop the rest of the cabbage. Spread the chopped cabbage over the bottom of the slow cooker. In a bowl, combine the meat, raw rice, egg, onion, carrot, and salt. Spread a portion of this mixture in the center of each of the large cabbage leaves, leaving a generous flap on either side. Roll up the leaves, sausage fashion. Place the rolls in the slow cooker, tucking the flap ends in neatly as you set the rolls down. In a small bowl, combine the vinegar, brown sugar, and tomato sauce and pour over the rolls. Cover and cook on Low for 6 to 8 hours.
Makes 4 to 6 servings.

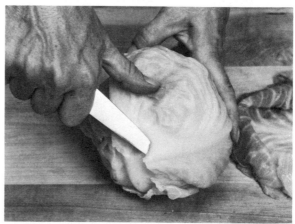

Removing outer leaves from parboiled cabbage before stuffing is easy when you use a sharp knife to cut them free from central core.

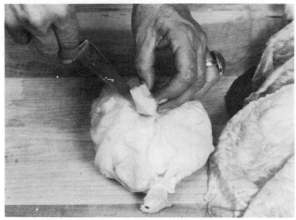
Removing central core facilitates removal of inner leaves.

Stuffing the center of the cabbage leaves. Place a small mound of stuffing near the curled-up stem end; roll the end over to cover the mound and tuck the leading edge in firmly. Fold each side of the leaf over and continue rolling the stuffed form up firmly, sausage-fashion.

Neatly rolled-up cabbage leaves are set, bottom-flap down, on a bed of cut-up parboiled cabbage, then cooked in a rich tomato sauce.

Vegetable Marmite
8 to 10 hours

A mélange of vegetables that gives off a wonderful home-cooking smell and is almost effortless to prepare.

6 medium potatoes, peeled and thinly sliced	1 onion, thinly sliced
	¼ cup raw rice
	1 tsp. salt
1 small turnip, peeled and diced	⅛ tsp. pepper
	⅛ tsp. allspice
1 cup fresh or frozen peas	2 cups beef bouillon, or Steero granules in 2 cups water
2 large tomatoes, skinned and quartered	

To Cook: In the slow pot layer the vegetables, ending with the rice and seasoning. Pour the beef consommé over the vegetables. Cover and cook on Low for 8 to 10 hours. Makes 6 servings.

Cabbage, Apples, and Potatoes Casserole
3 to 4 hours

A hearty dish for winter dinners, it uses up leftover mashed potatoes — and it's good and inexpensive besides.

3 Tbs. butter	2 Tbs. granulated sugar
2 medium onions, peeled and chopped	2 tsp. salt
	¼ tsp. pepper
1 small head of white cabbage, shredded	2 cups chicken bouillon or Steero chicken granules in 2 cups hot water
2 green apples, thinly sliced	
1½ tsp. white vinegar	½ cup leftover mashed potatoes

To Cook: In a large skillet, over medium heat, melt the butter and simmer the onions until golden brown. In the slow cooker make alternate layers of cabbage and apple. Add the vinegar, sugar, salt, and pepper. Mix the chicken bouillon into the mashed potatoes to make a thin sauce and pour it over the cabbage. Cover and bake on High for 3 to 4 hours. Makes 6 to 7 servings.

Casserole of Root Vegetables
6 to 8 hours

This takes a long time to cook, and the vegetables won't be a very pretty color when they're finished, but they taste very good with pork roasts and game dishes.

4 Tbs. butter	2 tsp. salt
2 cups peeled, diced white turnips	¼ tsp. black pepper
2 cups scraped, diced carrots	½ tsp. oregano (optional)
2 cups peeled, diced white potatoes	1 cup water

To Cook: Butter the bottom and sides of the slow cooker. Combine the diced vegetables with the salt and pepper and oregano and turn into the cooker. Add the water. Cover and cook on Low for 6 to 8 hours, or until tender.
Makes 6 to 8 servings.

Papa's Scalloped Potatoes
3 to 4 hours

3 Tbs. butter	2 tsp. salt
4 large potatoes, peeled and sliced ¼ inch thick	¼ tsp. pepper
	½ cup light cream or whole milk

To Cook: Butter the bottom and sides of the slow pot. Arrange a row of sliced potatoes, season with salt and pepper, and add half the remaining butter. Repeat. Add the cream. Cover and cook on High for 3 to 4 hours.
Makes 4 servings.

Turnip and Carrot Pot
6 to 8 hours

A long-cooking winter dish that makes a great accompaniment for roast duck.

3 Tbs. butter	¼ tsp. salt
2 cups peeled, diced white turnips	1 tsp. strained lemon juice
2 cups scraped, diced carrots	

To Cook: Butter the sides and bottom of the slow cooker. Combine the vegetables with the salt and turn into the cooker. Cover and cook on Low for 6 to 8 hours.

Before Serving: If there's liquid in the bottom of the cooker, turn the heat to High and cook uncovered until the liquid has gone. Sprinkle lemon juice over the vegetables, toss well, and serve.
Makes 4 to 6 servings.

9
Side Dishes

The slow cooker is a real help in preparing meals that have grains and grits and beans as a basis. Let the beans or grains cook overnight while you sleep. In the morning you can begin the second half of the dinner. The end result is a meal that normally would take hours of kitchen time made with very little investment of time on your part. Typical is Polenta with Meat Sauce. Here you do the cornmeal that is the basis of the polenta overnight in the slow cooker, and in the morning, while the polenta firms in its ring mold, you put the slow cooker to work on the meat sauce.

Baked Beans is a dish that never cooks without drying out when you do it in anything but a slow cooker. The beans, as described below, are tricky to get right in a slow cooker until you have experience with the timing for your cooker. This is more true with beans than with any other ingredient, because beans seem to be very individualistic about how quickly or slowly they will cook, whatever the cooker. It probably has to do with the way they grew, the year they were dried. And, too, with how old they are.

An interest in baked beans can lead you to a whole world of dried legumes, a world the slow cooker makes yours. Standing around while lentils or dried split peas for a puree are cooking to make sure the water doesn't dry out can be tedious. With a slow cooker, it's a snap.

Beans and Dried Vegetables

Beans and dried vegetables are specialties of the slow cooker, but you have to understand your beans and know what you are doing. Red beans that haven't been soaked can take 24 hours to soften in a slow cooker — in my experience, they are the slowest to cook. Some slow cookers will cook them more quickly than that. I've experimented with several types and concluded that this is an area where you'd best experiment for yourself. Test-cook one cupful of beans in 3 cups of water overnight and see at what point the following day they are really cooked through and delicious. Red beans, navy beans, chick peas, and other types of beans all cook at different times and actually vary from lot to lot to some extent. That's why many slow-cook recipes including beans suggest you use canned beans.

Beans and Dried Vegetables   *Lima beans, lentils, red beans, split peas, chick peas, and rice are among the legumes and grains that the slow-cook pot does superbly. Cooked from scratch — rather than taken from a can — the old-fashioned ingredients are really flavorful, and they can be served with, or included in, a wide range of delicious, inexpensive dishes. Excellent source of protein.*

However, canned beans never can taste like dried beans you've cooked yourself, so it's worth getting the hang of your cooker's ways with beans and then cooking yours from scratch. Cooking your own beans from scratch makes beans a really economical food, too. They're very inexpensive dried and relatively expensive canned.

Dried lima beans, split peas, lentils, and mixed dried vegetables done in a slow cooker have very rich flavors and bring a wonderful new variety to the vegetable scene, particularly in winter. We're used to using them in soups, but they make excellent side dishes to serve with meats and casseroles as well. Try some of the recipes here and then improvise your own. The rule of thumb for adding water is to use twice as much water as you have measured dried vegetables — but this is an indication rather than a hard-and-fast rule; some absorb more water than others. However, if the

vegetables need more water than was included in the slow pot, they won't burn. If you come to a potful of still-hard dried vegetables, simply add more water and turn the heat to High until they are cooked.

The recipes for Puree of Peas and Casserole of Lentils are basic to cooking this type of dried legume. Experiment with these, then adapt the results of these recipes to your own favorite dinners. They can become an adjunct for your family's preferred roast and stewed meats. Combine lentils and Chili con Carne, for instance. They go well together. Chili powder, Tabasco sauce, and any other favorite condiment can bring back an old and favored taste. Puree of Peas can become an elegant garnish for a baked ham.

Cereals and Grains

A slow cooker produces that wonder of wonders — perfectly cooked rice every time — as long as it is converted rice. Since converted rice is thought by many nutritionists to be the most nutritious, you may as well use it. Converted rice can (I've done it) cook at Low for 8 to 10 hours in the slow cooker that really cooks slowly and sit covered a couple of hours more without becoming mushy. Because the slow cooker cooks rice so perfectly, dishes of vegetables and rice — pilafs — are good candidates for slow cooking.

There are wonderful cereals we've lost the habit of serving regularly. Wheat, rye, and barley are among them, and they make delicious replacements for rice with casseroles and richly sauced dishes. Cooked in a slow pot, they are textured, nutty in flavor, and a delight to eat. I cook them in twice their volume of water plus half a cup and add salt and butter at the end.

The same cereals can cook all night in a slow cooker and make wonderful breakfast food when sweetened and served with whole milk or cream.

The Pastas

Spaghetti and noodles and macaroni aren't particularly good ingredients to cook in a slow pot. Cook these in rapidly boiling salted water on the top of the stove, then combine with your slow-cooked ingredients.

Corn Pudding
3 or 4 hours

A great corn dish you can make while you are away if you have a crockery cooker large enough to hold a 1½-quart baking dish and a trivet.

2 cups whole corn kernels, fresh or canned, drained	⅛ tsp. nutmeg
	2 Tbs. sifted all-purpose flour
4 egg yolks	1 tsp. baking powder
1 tsp. salt	2 Tbs. melted butter
⅛ tsp. pepper	2 cups scalded milk or 1 cup of evaporated milk
1 tsp. sugar	
½ green pepper, seeded and minced	4 egg whites
	4 cups hot water

To Cook: In the blender, blend the corn at low speed, drain, and turn the corn solids into a large bowl. Discard the liquid. Beat the egg yolks until thick and lemon colored. Beat in the corn, salt, pepper, sugar, green pepper, and nutmeg. Beat the flour and baking powder into the egg mixture, then beat in the melted butter. Finally, beat in the scalded milk. Beat the egg whites until stiff and fold into the corn mixture. Turn the pudding into a 1½-quart baking dish and cover with a lid or with foil. Set a metal rack or trivet in the bottom of the slow cooker. Pour 4 cups of hot water into the cooker, and set the baking dish on the trivet. Cover the pot and cook on High about 3 or 4 hours, or until a silver knife inserted in the middle comes out clean.
Makes 6 to 8 servings.

Foolproof Rice
6 to 8 hours

What a slow cooker can do with rice is unbelievable! The rice literally can cook for hours and hours and stay perfect. Even after it's done, it stays perfect if left in the pot.

1 cup converted rice	1 Tbs. butter or vegetable oil
2 cups water	
2 tsp. salt	

To Cook: Place all the ingredients together in the slow pot, cover, and cook on Low for 6 to 8 hours.
Makes 2 to 4 servings.

Rice and Parsley Casserole
6 to 8 hours

This variation on plain rice will give you ideas on other ways to dress up this staple cereal. It is a very good way to fix rice to be served with plain roasted meats.

1 cup converted rice	2 large cloves garlic, peeled, and minced
2 cups water	
2 tsp. salt	½ cup finely minced parsley
3 Tbs. butter	

To Cook: Place all the ingredients except the garlic, parsley, and half the butter together in the slow pot, cover, and cook on Low for 6 to 8 hours.
Before Serving: In a large skillet, melt the remaining butter and, over medium heat, sauté the garlic for one minute. Add the rice and mix it well with the garlic. Sprinkle the parsley over the top and stir and mix into the rice. Serve hot.
Makes 2 to 4 servings.

Rice with Mushrooms and Onions
6 to 8 hours

1 cup converted rice	½ cup fresh mushrooms, wiped and coarsely chopped
2 cups water	
2 tsp. salt	
3 Tbs. butter	
	1 large onion, peeled and finely minced

To Cook: Place all ingredients except onion and mushrooms and half the butter in the slow pot, cover, and cook on Low for 6 to 8 hours.
Before Serving: In a large skillet, melt remaining butter and, over medium heat, sauté the onion until translucent. Add the mushrooms and sauté until all moisture is gone, for 3 or 4 minutes. Add the rice and mix well with the onions and mushrooms. Serve hot.
Makes 2 to 4 servings.

Polenta with Meat Sauce
8 to 10 hours

Cornmeal is a breakfast cereal in New England, but elsewhere it is also the basis for main-course side dishes. Polenta, an Italian specialty, begins with cornmeal. Start the cornmeal the night before, let it set during the day, and you are ready to fry it for a side dish for Italian foods that evening.

Cornmeal, cooked, cooled, and served with Slow-Pot Meat Sauce, makes a complete dinner, and one children love.

1½ cups cornmeal	1 recipe Slow-Pot
3 cups water	Meat Sauce
1 tsp. salt	(page 36)
1 Tbs. butter	

To Cook: Combine cornmeal and 2 cups of water in the slow cooker. Mix well. Stir in remaining water and salt. Cover and cook on Low for 8 to 10 hours, or until so thick a spoon will stand in it. Pour into a buttered 1½-quart ring mold and let cool.

Before Serving: Slice the polenta and place around a large serving platter. Fill the center of the platter with Slow-Pot Meat Sauce. Serve one or two pieces of polenta to each diner and spoon Slow-Pot Meat Sauce over the pieces. Makes 8 servings.

Baked Beans
18 to 20 hours

Start this the day before. The beans take a lot of cooking, but since the cooker cooks for just pennies a day, in the end the beans you make yourself will cost lots less, and they'll taste lots better. Soak the beans before cooking.

1 lb. dry navy beans, soaked overnight	3 medium onions, peeled and quartered
3⅓ cups water	¼ cup tightly packed brown sugar
1⅔ cups evaporated milk	¼ cup dark molasses
2 tsp. dry mustard	2 Tbs. vinegar
¼ tsp. pepper	⅛ tsp. cinnamon
1 Tbs. salt	⅛ tsp. ground cloves
¼ lb. salt pork	½ tsp. pepper

Baked Beans

To Cook: Soak the beans the day before and cook on Low overnight in 3 cups of water. Drain the water. Return the beans to the cooker with remaining ingredients. Cover and cook on Low for 10 to 12 hours. Makes 4 to 6 servings

Lentils Served with Frankfurters

Casserole of Lentils
8 to 10 hours

Dried lentils are small, meaty legumes, dark brown in color, with a nutty flavor all their own. They are good with strongly flavored meats, such as frankfurters. As they are one of the most nourishing of all the legumes, nutrition buffs will love this.

2 cups dried lentils, well washed	2 cups water
	2 tsp. salt
4 frankfurters, cut into 1-inch pieces	½ tsp. marjoram
	½ tsp. sugar
1 stalk celery, cut into ¼-inch slices	4 Tbs. butter

To Cook: Place all the ingredients except the butter in the slow cooker, cover, and cook on Low for 8 to 10 hours or until lentils are completely soft.

Before Serving: If any cooking liquid remains, turn heat to High and simmer, uncovered, until the moisture is gone. Beat the butter into the lentils and serve.

Makes 8 to 10 servings.

Puree of Peas

Puree of Peas
8 to 10 hours

This is different — a puree of dried green peas on the lines of a popular French dish, Purée St. Germain.

2 cups dried split green peas, well washed	2 tsp. salt
	½ tsp. dill
	1 large bay leaf
2 cups water or 1 cup evaporated milk	½ tsp. sugar
	4 Tbs. butter

To Cook: Place all the ingredients except the butter in the slow cooker, cover, and cook on Low for 8 to 10 hours or until peas are completely soft.

Before Serving: If any cooking liquid remains, turn heat to High and simmer, uncovered, until the excess moisture is gone. Discard the bay leaf. Beat the butter into the peas and serve.

Makes 8 to 10 servings.

Rye Berries
8 to 12 hours

This is whole-grain rye — a delicious substitute for wild rice, brown rice, or plain rice. The cooking time for cereals such as this seems to vary tremendously among slow cookers. So the first time you cook it in your electric crockery pot, plan to check on doneness every few hours.

1 cup rye berries	1 small onion, peeled and chopped
2 cups water	
1 tsp. salt	3 Tbs. butter

To Cook: Place all ingredients except the butter in the slow cooker; cover and cook on Low for 8 to 12 hours.

Before Serving: Place in a serving dish, dot with butter, and let the butter melt over the berries before serving.

Makes 4 to 5 servings.

Wheat Berries
8 to 12 hours

These are a bit less nutty than the rye berries but very good.

1 cup wheat berries	1 small onion, peeled and chopped
2 cups water	
1 tsp. salt	3 Tbs. butter

To Cook: Place all ingredients except the butter in the slow cooker; cover and cook on Low for 8 to 12 hours.

Before Serving: Place in a serving dish, dot with butter, and let the butter melt over the berries before serving.

Makes 4 to 5 servings.

Wheat Berry Breakfast
Follow the recipe for cooking Wheat Berries above. Let the berries cook overnight and in the morning serve them with half-and-half (or milk), sugar, and chopped fruit or blueberries.

Rye Berry Breakfast

Follow the recipe for cooking Rye Berries (page 79). Let the berries cook overnight and in the morning serve with half-and-half (or milk) and brown sugar or honey or corn syrup.

Barley Casserole
8 to 12 hours

A change from rice — and very good with lamb and middle-European dishes.

1 cup barley	1 small onion, peeled
2 cups water	and chopped
1 tsp. salt	3 Tbs. butter

To Cook: Place all ingredients except the butter in the slow cooker; cover and cook on Low for 8 to 12 hours.

Before Serving: Place in a serving dish, dot with butter, and let the butter melt over the barley before serving.
Makes 4 to 5 servings.

Bean Casserole Sablaise
20 to 24 hours

This is one of the best side dishes for lamb, and it is wonderful when done very slowly in an electric crockery pot. It is strongly flavored with garlic. Do you like garlic? Start the dish the night before.

2 cups dried small white beans, soaked 4 hours	2 tsp. salt
	4 large cloves garlic, peeled
4 cups water	½ tsp. black pepper
⅛ lb. salt pork, cut into chunks	

To Cook: Place all the ingredients in the cooker, cover, and cook on Low until the following night at dinner.
Makes 6 to 8 servings.

Part V
Comfort Foods
and Desserts

10
Baking and Sweets to Slow Cook

You can tell a comfort food right away because it always has a lot of calories and you always feel guilty as you prepare it. And the family always groans with pleasure when its aroma materializes in and near the kitchen. Whether it's bread, corn bread, muffins, carrot tea bread, pumpkin bread, or plum pudding, there's no denying the calories involved — especially when you load them down with butter and jam or use them to sop up rich gravies.

However, you do not live by the shape of your figure alone. And sometimes — after a skating party or a hard day's work in the garden — you've actually burned up enough calories to be able to face Irish Bread without a tremor.

Baking in a Slow Cooker

As mentioned before, under some circumstances (when it is cooking stews and casseroles and braising meats, for instance) a slow cooker acts as a Dutch oven. But at other times it can be like a small real oven or a steamer. Because it uses up so few energy-pennies a day, it is economical to use for baking small quantities. Baking in an oven, unless you really need lots of space, heats a large area when a smaller one would do. If things baked in your slow cooker don't come out just right the first time, experiment a little, and eventually you'll turn out surprisingly handsome baked goods. Test one or two recipes here in your baking equipment — you may want to halve some of the recipes.

To do much baking in a slow cooker, you must have one of the larger units. The low, small units can't handle much. But it is fun to try half recipes in them, and all the other recipes in this section can be halved and cooked in smaller units.

Some of the manufacturers — notably Rival — are marketing baking units that fit inside slow cookers. If your slow cooker isn't equipped with a baking utensil, you can easily improvise. Study the commercial baking units offered, and you'll see they are tall so that doughs can rise high. They are lidded to keep the steam, which forms inside the cover of the slow cooker, from falling back into the batter or dough. Below the lid, there are vents in the sides of the container so that steam from the cooking batter can escape into the slow pot. A

Baking in a Slow Cooker *Baking unit in foreground is made expressly for crock pot and doesn't fit all makes. You can easily improvise baking units with items as simple as a 2-pound coffee can, Pyrex cups or casseroles that fit your particular brand of slow cooker. Note shapes of the many baked goods the slow cooker does well; all are tall cakes, an unusual form that adds to the fun of cooking your own comfort foods the slow way.*

Other Baking Units *Some substitutes for a commercial baking pot: in foreground, 3-quart casserole, or soufflé dish; to the right, a 1½-quart soufflé dish topped by glass lid; background container is a loosely lidded 1½-quart crock. Note twists of foil that will vent the interior of baking container. Pyrex cup under the 3-quart dish serves as a rack when placed in bottom of the slow-cook pot used for baking.*

cover to keep steam from falling into the batter and venting to let steam out of the cooking utensil are the essential elements in baking improvisations. A two-pound coffee can is a good substitute.

Muffin tins don't fit slow cookers. However, Pyrex muffin cups do. I make a double-decker layer of them, using Pyrex cups or a plate to cover the bottom layer and a piece of foil to keep steam from the top layer. About 6 Pyrex muffin cups, each 2½ inches across, fit several of the slow-cooker models on the market — making half the average recipe. (If you have mixed up a batch of ingredients and find it doesn't fit the intended baking equipment, cook in a mold, as described on page 84.)

Pyrex Baking Cups *Pyrex baking cups make a good substitute for muffin tins when the muffins are to be made in the slow cooker. Second set of Pyrex cups top the baking units, keeping the muffin mix free of steam drops and creating a shelf for stacking a second layer of muffins.*

Top deck of muffins in place. These can be sheltered from steam droplets by covering with a sheet of loosely placed foil.

Foil Cap and Vent Twist *A small twist of the foil (in the right hand), inserted between cooker lid and cooker rim, allows little heat to escape but vents enough steam to reduce condensation within cooker when it is used as a baking oven. Muffin cups stacked within cooker are topped here with a foil cap to keep moisture droplets from falling into batter.*

Top deck of muffins can be protected by foil muffin cups instead of foil sheet. The important thing is to keep the droplets of steam that condense on the cooker lid from falling into the batter.

One thing you'll find helpful for baking is a trivet or a metal rack. If your cooker doesn't come equipped with one, measure the cooker's diameter and buy one, or use a Pyrex cup, as illustrated. In my experience, breads and cakes are more successful when they sit a little above the floor of the slow cooker than when they sit right on it.

About Baking Recipes

When you are baking in a slow cooker, prepare the dough or batter as you would when cooking in conventional utensils; then pour the batter or place the dough in a container the right size to fit inside your slow cooker. The large cookers will take 1-, 1½-, and 2- or 3-quart molds. The molds' high sides are important. The dough or batter needs space to rise under a cover. Since molds don't come equipped with covers or lids, use a plate or piece of foil to cover the mold and to keep steam from dampening the dough. A mold can sit on a Pyrex cup if you have no trivet.

Custards cook beautifully in soufflé dish or casserole. This is the 1½-quart size, topped with a loosely placed foil lid to keep condensing steam from falling into custard. Note Pyrex cup to be used as a rack on the floor of the slow cooker; crumpled foil pressed over the upended bottom stabilizes the casserole resting on top.

Some doughs and batters don't need to be protected from the steam — for instance, Plum Pudding is steamed rather than baked. Other batters are dense enough to take all the steam likely to fall on them without harm. But other batters, such as Pound Cake, should be kept away from steam.

Moist cakes and tea breads come out very well in the slow cooker. And you'll find it is fun to experiment with making homemade breads of all sorts from scratch. Among the recipes that follow are some basic combinations. Use these to adapt your own favorite recipes for fruit breads, yeast breads, and buns.

Using the Timer for Baking

While some baked goods turn out well cooked on Low, many of the recipes call for cooking on High for just a few hours (not 8 to 10 hours!). Mix your batter and use a timer to start the slow pot going in your absence. That lets you leave whenever you like and come back to the aroma of ready-to-eat muffins or cake. If you delay baking goods containing baking powder and baking soda, they may end up flatter than they should be. This may be because the baking powder or baking soda warmed up as soon as the ingredients were mixed and had lost its rising power by the time baking began. Keep all the ingredients cooled when you time your baking to start several hours after the batter has been mixed. If the recipes call for water in the slow cooker before baking starts, add an equivalent of ice cubes for timer-started baking.

You won't get the kind of richly browned tops on goods baked in slow cookers that you get in an oven. Icing or glaze will mask that for party occasions. But in truth it's such a treat to have comfort foods without seeing the cook slaving over the stove for an hour before it is served that no one will mind much.

Don't Lift the Lid During Baking

During the early part of the baking, don't lift the lid. You will let out heat and delay the baking process. When the baked goods are almost done, lift the lid and test quickly for doneness by inserting a toothpick in the center of the cake or bread.

Breakfast Foods

Whole cereals and grains make wonderful breakfast foods and nearly all of them can be cooked overnight in the slow cooker. Try these on family members who hate to eat in the morning. The texture of Cornmeal Mush swimming in butter and the nutty flavor of Rye Berries in milk or cream appeal to palates jaded by cornflakes. After such a hearty breakfast, you won't find yourself dying for a candy bar or a coffee cake halfway through the morning. There are some basic recipes for cooking whole grains in Chapter 9. They make clear how to adapt slow cooking to the cooking of similar breakfast foods. A good source for glamorous cereals are the health food stores.

Puddings, Custards, and Compotes

Some other breakfast foods from Grandmother's day are stewed dried fruits such as prunes, raisins, and apricots. These (as well as fresh fruits) can be cooked overnight in the cooker and be ready to eat when you get up. Or they can be cooked overnight and chilled all day, to provide economical and richly nutritious desserts for dinner. In many areas, electrical rates are lower at night than during the day. In these areas, overnight cooking has a double appeal: you rise to a delicious breakfast at half the price!

Custards and puddings respond beautifully to the slow, gentle heat of the slow cooker. Some require covering to keep steam from the ingredients. I've included two basic rice pudding recipes that will give you an idea of what the cooker can do in this area. Caramel Custard — one of the world's favorite desserts — also turns out well in a slow cooker.

Basic White Bread
2 to 3 hours

2 cups lukewarm water
1 package dry yeast
1 Tbs. granulated sugar
3½ cups unrefined flour or all-purpose flour
½ tsp. salt
2 Tbs. oil
Milk

To Cook: Preheat the slow pot on High with the lid on. Dissolve the yeast in ½ cup of the lukewarm water with the sugar and set in a warm — not hot — place. Put the flour in a large bowl and sprinkle with the salt. Make a well in the center. When the yeast is bubbly, pour the rest of the water, the yeast mixture, and the oil into the well. Stir with your fingers until all the flour has been absorbed. Grease a 2-quart mold and place the bread in it. Brush milk with a pastry brush over the top of the bread. Cover loosely with a plate and let stand for 5 minutes in a warm place. Place on a trivet in the slow cooker, cover the cooker, and bake on High for 2 to 3 hours.
Makes 1 loaf.

Carrot Tea Bread

Carrot Tea Bread
2½ to 3½ hours

This is a New England favorite. You can top it with a sugar and milk glaze or frost it with your favorite vanilla frosting mix.

1 cup all-purpose flour
1 cup granulated sugar
1 tsp. baking powder
½ tsp. salt
1 tsp. ground cinnamon
2 whole eggs
½ cup vegetable oil
4 cups raw grated carrots (about 4 medium carrots)
½ cup chopped pecans

To Cook: Measure the flour, sugar, baking powder, salt, and cinnamon into a sifter. Sift three times into a medium bowl. With an electric beater, beat the eggs until frothy and lemon colored. Toward the end, dribble in the oil. With the beater on low, add the flour mixture a little at a time. Fold in the carrots and pecans. Pour into a well-greased and floured 2-quart mold. Place in the slow cooker; cover loosely with a plate. Cover the cooker, but prop the lid open a fraction with a toothpick or a twist of foil to let excess steam escape. Bake on High for 2½ to 3½ hours, or until a toothpick inserted in the center comes out clean.
Makes 6 to 8 servings.

Pumpkin Butter Bread
2½ to 3 hours

This is really best made with butter. Serve it warm with more butter. Toast, refrigerate, or freeze leftovers.

1½ cups all-purpose flour
½ tsp. salt
½ tsp. baking soda
½ tsp. baking powder
¼ tsp. cinnamon
¼ tsp. ground ginger
¼ tsp. grated nutmeg
2 eggs
1 cup granulated sugar
1 cup drained pumpkin
¾ cup melted butter
½ cup chopped nuts

To Cook: Sift the flour, salt, baking soda, baking powder, cinnamon, ground ginger, and grated nutmeg together into a large bowl. With an electric beater, whip the eggs until frothy; add the sugar gradually as you beat. With the beater on low, beat in the well-drained pumpkin (make sure there's as little moisture as possible left in the pumpkin) and the melted butter. Whip in the flour mixture, then fold in the chopped nuts. Pour into a 1-quart mold and cover with a loosely fitting plate. Set on a trivet or rack in the bottom of the slow cooker. Cover the cooker, but prop the lid open a fraction with a toothpick or a twist of foil to let excess steam escape. Cook on High for 2½ to 3 hours. When a toothpick inserted in the center of the cake comes out clean, it is done.

Makes 4 to 6 servings.

Date Nut Bread

Date Nut Bread
2½ to 3 hours

This is on the sweet side but awfully good. Children love it for breakfast or for afternoon snacks. Wrapped and refrigerated, it will keep fresh for several days, or you can freeze leftovers.

¾ cup walnut meats	1 cup granulated
1 cup pitted dates	sugar
½ cup sifted all-purpose flour	2 Tbs. dark corn syrup
3 Tbs. shortening	1 cup sifted all-purpose flour
¾ cup boiling water	
2 eggs	1½ tsp. baking soda
1 tsp. vanilla	½ tsp. salt

To Cook: Chop the walnut meats coarsely with a knife (the blender tends to make them into mush). Place the dates on a chopping board, sprinkle the ½ cup of flour over them, and chop them. If you keep the dates well mixed with the flour, they won't stick to the knife as you work. Place the dates in a colander and shake the colander over the chopping board to remove as much flour as possible. Place the dates in a bowl, add the shortening and the boiling water, and let them stand as you prepare the batter. Beat the eggs well with a fork, add the vanilla, sugar, and corn syrup. Scoop all the flour from the chopping board and combine it with 1 cup of flour, the baking soda, and the salt. Beat the flour mixture into the eggs. Add the date mixture and beat just enough to blend all the ingredients. Fold in the nuts. Pour into a greased, floured, 1-quart mold. Cover with a loosely fitting plate. Set the mold on a trivet or rack in the slow cooker. Cover the cooker, but prop the lid open a fraction with a toothpick or a twist of foil to let excess steam escape. Cook on High for 2½ to 3 hours. Cool the bread on a rack for 10 minutes, then unmold. Serve warm.

Makes 4 to 6 servings.

Apple Cake
3 to 4 hours

1 cup sifted all-purpose flour	4 cups sliced, pared, cored tart apples
1½ tsp. baking powder	½ tsp. cinnamon
½ tsp. salt	¼ tsp. nutmeg
1 Tbs. granulated sugar	2 Tbs. granulated sugar
¼ cup shortening	½ cup apricot jam
1 whole egg, slightly beaten	2 Tbs. melted butter
¼ cup milk	

To Cook: In a medium-large bowl, sift together the flour, baking powder, salt, and 1 tablespoon granulated sugar. With two knives, cut the shortening into the flour until mixture is mealy. Make a well in the center and drop in the egg and milk. Stir in the flour mixture to form smooth batter; turn into greased 2-quart mold. Arrange the apples in rows on top, pushing them halfway into the dough. In a small bowl, mix the cinnamon, nutmeg and 2 tablespoons sugar. Sprinkle over the apples and dot with apricot jam. Drizzle butter over all. Place in the slow cooker and cover loosely with a plate. Cover the cooker, but prop the lid open a fraction with a toothpick or a twist of foil to let excess steam escape. Cook on High for 3 to 4 hours.

Makes 6 servings.

Apricot Nut Bread
2 to 3 hours

¾ cup dried apricots	1 egg, slightly beaten
1 cup sifted all-purpose flour	1 Tbs. grated orange rind
2 tsp. baking powder	1 Tbs. vegetable oil
¼ tsp. baking soda	½ cup sifted whole wheat flour
½ tsp. salt	1 cup walnut meats, coarsely chopped
½ cup granulated sugar	
¾ cup milk	

To Cook: Place the dried apricots on a chopping block. Measure the all-purpose flour and sprinkle 1 tablespoon of it over the apricots. Dip the cutting knife into the flour and chop the apricots finely. Flour the knife often to keep the cut-up fruits from sticking together. Sift the remaining all-purpose flour, baking powder, baking soda, salt, and granulated sugar together into a large bowl. Combine the milk, egg, orange rind, and vegetable oil. Stir in the flour mixture and the whole wheat flour. Fold in the cut-up apricots, any flour left on the cutting block, and the walnut meats. Pour into a well-greased, floured, 1-quart mold. Cover with a loosely fitting plate and place on a rack or trivet in the slow cooker. Cover the cooker, but prop the lid open a fraction with a toothpick or a twist of foil to let excess steam escape. Cook on High for 2 to 3 hours. Cool on a rack for 10 minutes. Serve warm or cold.
Makes 4 to 6 servings.

Blueberry Muffins
2½ to 3 hours

These are my family's morning favorites. I use the timer to make these turn up ready for breakfast. You will need 6 large or 10 or 12 small Pyrex cups. Or make it as a bread in a soufflé dish. Mix half the recipe unless you have a very large cooker.

2 cups sifted all-purpose flour	1 cup whole milk
3 tsp. baking powder	6 Tbs. melted butter or vegetable oil
1 tsp. salt	1 cup washed, drained blueberries
2 Tbs. granulated sugar	3 Tbs. granulated sugar
1 egg, slightly beaten	

To Cook: Into a medium bowl, sift the flour, baking powder, salt, and 2 tablespoons sugar. Make a well in the center and pour in the egg, milk, and melted butter or oil. Stir together until mixed. Don't beat. Fold in the blueberries mixed with 3 tablespoons sugar. Divide the batter among the well-greased Pyrex cups, filling each only halfway. Place half the cups on a trivet in the bottom of the slow cooker. Set a Pyrex mold or pie plate over the cups to make room for a second layer of cups. Cover the top layer of cups loosely with a plate. Set the timer so that the muffins will start cooking on Low 2½ to 3 hours before breakfast time. If using muffin cups as described above, halve the recipe.
Makes 12 muffins.

Banana Bread

Banana Bread
2 to 3 hours

Banana Bread leftovers keep well in the refrigerator and can be sliced and toasted before serving again. Banana Bread also freezes well. Use overripe bananas for this — often they're on sale for very little.

1¾ cups sifted all-purpose flour	2 well-beaten eggs
2 tsp. baking powder	2 Tbs. dark corn syrup
¼ tsp. baking soda	1½ cups well-mashed, ripe bananas (2 or 3 bananas)
½ tsp. salt	
⅓ cup shortening	½ cup walnut meats (optional)
⅔ cup granulated sugar	

To Cook: Sift the flour, baking powder, baking soda, and salt together. With the electric beater on low, fluff the shortening until soft and creamy in a small bowl. Or beat by hand until fluffy. Add the sugar gradually. Beat in the eggs and dark corn syrup in a slow stream. With a fork, beat into the shortening a third of the bananas, half the flour, another third of the bananas, the remaining flour, and the last of the bananas. Fold in the walnut meats. Turn into a greased and floured 1½-quart mold and cover with a loosely fitting plate. Place the mold on a rack or a trivet in the cooker. Cover the cooker, but prop the lid open a fraction with a toothpick or a twist of foil to let excess steam escape. Cook on High for 2 to 3 hours, or until the bread is done. Cool on a rack for 10 minutes, then turn the bread out of the mold. Dust over with brown sugar and serve warm. Makes 6 to 8 servings.

Cranberry Bread
2½ to 3 hours

This is a Cape Cod specialty. In the restaurants there, a basket of sliced cranberry bread is served with each meal. It's best buttered and eaten fresh, but leftovers — toasted and buttered — make a wonderful breakfast food. Cranberry Bread freezes well and keeps fresh for many days in the refrigerator if well wrapped in plastic.

2 cups (½ lb.) fresh cranberries	6 Tbs. butter at room temperature
2 cups all-purpose flour	1 whole egg
1 cup granulated sugar	1 Tbs. grated orange peel
½ tsp. baking powder	½ cup orange juice
½ tsp. baking soda	½ cup walnut meats, chopped
½ tsp. salt	

To Cook: A quarter cup at a time, chop the cranberries in the blender on low. Don't puree them, which is what will happen if you blend them too long. In a large bowl, sift the flour, sugar, baking powder, baking soda, and salt. With two knives, cut the butter into the flour mixture until it looks like coarse meal. Combine the egg, orange peel, and orange juice and stir into the flour mixture until well blended. Fold in the cranberries and the walnut meats. Turn into a greased 2-quart mold. Cover with a loosely fitting plate. Place the mold on a rack or trivet in the slow cooker. Cover the cooker, but prop the lid open a fraction with a toothpick or a twist of foil to let excess steam escape. Cook on High for 2½ to 3 hours. Bread is done when a toothpick inserted in the center comes out clean. Cool the bread on a rack for 10 minutes, then unmold. Serve warm. Makes 5 to 6 servings.

Ruth Macguire's Soda Bread
2 hours

This soda bread recipe came to Ruth from an Irish friend via Brooklyn, but it is authentically Irish. You can glaze it with a runny mixture of sugar and milk set to firm up and dry in a low oven — 350° F. Irish restaurants in New York always offer warm soda bread with dinner, but they don't glaze it.

1½ cups sifted all-purpose flour	1 tsp. caraway seeds
1¼ tsp. baking powder	½ cup seedless raisins
¼ tsp. baking soda	2 tsp. shortening
½ tsp. salt	1 egg, slightly beaten
1½ Tbs. granulated sugar	1 cup buttermilk

To Cook: Sift the flour, baking powder, baking soda, salt, and sugar into a large bowl. Add the caraway seeds and raisins. Working with your fingers, rub the shortening into the flour mixture. Or with two knives, cut it into the flour until it makes a coarse mealy mixture. Add the egg and buttermilk and stir until you have formed a soft dough. Flour a board and turn the batter out onto it. Knead the dough lightly for one minute. Form a round loaf and make a shallow cross in the center. Place the dough in a well-floured 2-quart mold and cover loosely with a plate. Cover the cooker and bake on High for about 2 hours, or until the bread is crusty on top and a toothpick inserted in the center comes out clean. Makes 4 to 6 servings.

Boston Brown Bread
3 to 4 hours

This is great with baked beans and franks. It's dark and dense, and leftovers make wonderful toast.

1 cup whole wheat flour	1½ tsp. salt
1 cup rye flour	¾ cup dark molasses
1 cup yellow cornmeal	1½ cups buttermilk
2 tsp. baking soda	1 cup seedless raisins
	2 cups hot water

To Cook: In a large bowl, combine the whole wheat and rye flour, cornmeal, baking soda, and salt. Make a well in the center and pour in the molasses, buttermilk, and raisins. Stir until all the ingredients are combined. Grease a 2-quart mold, flour it, and fill. The batter should not fill more than ⅔ of the mold. Cover with foil and tie with string. Set the mold on a trivet in the bottom of the slow cooker. Pour the hot water into the pot, cover the pot, and cook on High for 3 to 4 hours. The bread is done when the top is dry and recedes from the edge of the mold. Cool the bread on a rack for 10 minutes, then turn out and serve.
Makes 1 loaf.

Corn Bread from Scratch
2 to 3 hours

Corn bread mix is so successful you really don't need to make it from scratch, but it costs more than a hand-mixed version. I grease the mold for corn bread with bacon drippings.

1¼ cups all-purpose flour	1 tsp. salt
¾ cup yellow cornmeal	1 egg, slightly beaten
¼ cup granulated sugar	1 cup milk
4½ tsp. baking powder	⅓ cup melted butter or vegetable oil

To Cook: In a medium bowl, sift together the flour, cornmeal, sugar, baking powder, and salt. Make a well in the center. Turn the egg, milk, and melted butter or oil into the well and beat into the dry mixture until just moistened. Turn into a greased 2-quart mold, cover with a plate, and place on a trivet or rack in the bottom of the slow cooker. Cover the cooker, cook on High for 2 to 3 hours.
Makes 6 servings.

Cornmeal Mush
6 to 8 hours

You can have cornmeal mush perfectly cooked and waiting when you get up.

½ cup cornmeal	3 cups water
½ tsp. salt	Butter
	Additional salt

To Cook: Place cornmeal, ½ tsp. salt, and water in the slow cooker and cover. Cook on Low for 6 to 8 hours.
Before Serving: Spoon into big cereal or soup plates and top with a tablespoon or two of butter. Offer salt with it rather than sugar. Many cooks cool the mush overnight, cut it into squares, fry it like pancakes, and serve it with maple syrup for breakfast.
Makes 4 to 6 servings.

Easy Orange Cake
2½ to 3½ hours

This is very nice with an orange butter icing — sweet butter whipped with confectioners' sugar and orange juice concentrate to which has been added 1 tablespoon of grated fresh orange rind.

1 package (16 oz.) pound cake mix	2 whole eggs
⅔ cup orange juice	3 Tbs. fresh grated orange rind

To Cook: Place the cake mix, orange juice, and eggs in a large bowl and beat by hand 300 times. Add the grated rind for the last round of beating. Pour the batter into a well-greased and floured 2-quart mold or spring-form pan. Place the pan in the slow cooker and cover with a loosely fitting plate. Cover the pot, but prop the lid open a fraction with a toothpick or a twist of foil to let excess steam escape. Cook on High for 2½ to 3½ hours. When a toothpick inserted in the center of the cake comes out clean, the cake is done. Cool on a rack for 10 minutes before turning the cake out of the pan.
Makes 10 to 12 servings.

Plum Pudding
5 to 6 hours

This recipe is a descendant of Ruth Macguire's great-grandmother's plum pudding — a traditional Christmas dinner dessert. It is flambéed with rum and served with a hard sauce on the side. Ruth makes it several weeks before Christmas and lets it ripen in a cool, dark closet, well wrapped in several thicknesses of cheesecloth soaked in rum and overwrapped with foil.

1 cup all-purpose flour	½ lb. unflavored dried bread crumbs
¾ tsp. salt	
½ tsp. baking powder	½ lb. beef suet, blended
½ Tbs. allspice	
2 tsp. ground ginger	½ lb. light brown sugar
¼ tsp. ground nutmeg	
½ lb. seedless dark raisins	3 medium apples, peeled, cored, and chopped fine
2 oz. candied citron peel	Grated rind of half a lemon
½ lb. dried currants	¼ cup dark rum
½ lb. golden seedless raisins	¼ cup apple cider
3 oz. slivered almonds	4 eggs, well beaten

To Cook: Sift the flour, salt, baking powder, allspice, ginger, and nutmeg into a very large bowl. Stir in the remaining ingredients one at a time until all are added. Grease a 2-quart pudding mold or a regular mold and pour mixture in. Cover with a square of clean linen and tie down the linen with string. Place on a trivet in a slow cooker and add 2 cups of water. Cover and cook on High for 5 to 6 hours.
Makes 10 to 12 servings.

Pound Cake from a Mix
2½ to 3½ hours

Real pound cake from scratch takes a pound of sugar, a pound of flour, and a pound of butter — which makes it really expensive today. The mix works beautifully, and costs lots less. It freezes beautifully.

1 package (16 oz.) pound cake mix	⅔ cup water
	2 whole eggs

To Cook: Turn the cake mix, water, and eggs into a large mixing bowl and beat by hand 300 times. Do it by hand — this give it a more from-scratch texture. Pour the batter into a greased and floured 2-quart mold or a spring-form pan. Set the pan in the slow cooker and cover the top with a loosely fitting plate. Cover the pot, but prop the lid open a fraction with a toothpick or a twist of foil to let excess steam escape. Cook on High for 2½ to 3½ hours. When a toothpick inserted in the center comes out clean, the cake is finished. Cool the cake on a rack for 10 minutes before you turn it out of the pan.
Makes 8 servings.

Cherry Pound Cake
2½ to 3½ hours

My mother used to make this from scratch, but it's much easier with a pound cake mix. Refrigerate leftovers wrapped in plastic film.

1 package (16 oz.) pound cake mix	20 or 30 maraschino cherries, drained
⅔ cup water	3 Tbs. all-purpose flour
2 whole eggs	

To Cook: Turn the cake mix, water, and eggs into a large mixing bowl and beat with an electric beater on low. In a small bowl, combine the maraschino cherries with the flour. Toss the cherries well in the flour so that all the moisture on the cherries is absorbed. Pour the batter into a greased and floured 2-quart mold or spring-form pan. Drop the cherries into the batter from high enough up so they sink into it. (This maneuver keeps all the cherries, which are heavier than the batter, from sinking to the bottom of the cake.) Place the pan in the slow cooker and cover with a loosely fitting plate. Cover the pot, but prop the lid open a fraction with a toothpick or a twist of foil to let excess steam escape. Cook on High for 2½ to 3½ hours. When a toothpick inserted in the center of the cake comes out clean, the cake is done. Cool the cake on a rack for 10 to 15 minutes before you turn it out of the pan. Let it cool thoroughly before serving.
Makes 10 to 12 servings.

Pineapple Pound Cake
2½ to 3½ hours

1 package (16 oz.) pound cake mix	2 whole eggs
⅔ cup pineapple juice drained from a 16-oz. can of pineapple tidbits	1½ cups pineapple tidbits
	3 Tbs. all-purpose flour

To Cook: Turn the cake mix, pineapple juice, and eggs into a large mixing bowl and beat with an electric beater on low. In a small bowl, combine the drained pineapple tidbits with the flour. Toss them well in the flour so that any moisture left over on the tidbits is absorbed. Fold the tidbits into the batter. Pour the batter into a greased and floured 2-quart mold or spring-form pan. Place the pan in the slow cooker and cover with a loosely fitting plate. Cover the pot, but prop the lid open a fraction with a toothpick or a twist of foil to let excess steam escape. Cook on High for 2½ to 3½ hours. When a toothpick inserted in the center of the cake comes out clean, the cake is done. Cool the cake on a rack for 10 or 15 minutes before you turn it out of the pan. Let it cool thoroughly before serving.
Makes 10 to 12 servings.

Caramel Custard
2 to 4 hours

A custard dessert to serve with caramel sauce. Make it a day ahead so it can be chilled or bake it overnight in your slow cooker and chill it until dinner.

4 medium eggs	4½ cups granulated sugar
1 tsp. vanilla	½ cup boiling water
3½ cups whole milk	

To Cook: Beat the eggs with an electric beater until thick. Add the vanilla and beat until lemon colored. Add the milk and 2½ cups of the sugar; with the beater on low, combine well. Butter a 2-quart mold. In a heavy medium-sized skillet melt the remaining 2 cups of sugar over a very low heat. When it begins to bubble and turn brown, stir to combine all the sugar in the skillet. When the caramelizing sugar is a medium brown, pour half the caramel into the bottom of the mold. Into the other half of the caramelized sugar in the skillet, pour ½ cup of boiling water. Stir over low heat until the mixture bubbles; allow it to cool, then chill for use as sauce. Pour the egg and milk mixture into the mold. Pour 2 cups of hot water into the slow cooker and place the mold on a trivet or rack in the bottom. Cover the pot, but prop the lid open a fraction with a toothpick or a twist of foil to allow excess steam to escape. Cook on High for 2 to 4 hours or until a silver knife inserted in the center of the custard comes out clean. Chill, covered, in the refrigerator, then unmold and serve with caramel sauce over the top.
Makes 6 to 8 servings.

Indian Pudding
2 to 3 hours

The slow cooker does this spicy cornmeal dessert beautifully. You can make it with half-and-half instead of milk if you want a rich pudding.

3½ cups cold whole milk	½ tsp. ground ginger
⅓ cup yellow cornmeal	1 tsp. ground cinnamon
2 eggs	4 Tbs. butter
¼ cup dark molasses	¾ cup golden seedless raisins
½ cup light brown sugar, firmly packed	½ pint light or heavy cream
½ tsp. salt	

To Cook: Over medium heat in a large saucepan, heat 3 cups of the milk. Combine the ½ cup cold milk with the cornmeal and turn into the saucepan. Stir continuously until the mixture begins to thicken. Lower the heat and stir 20 minutes more. Beat the eggs in a small bowl and stir in the molasses, sugar, salt, ginger, and cinnamon. Cut the butter into the cornmeal mixture and stir in the raisins. Add the egg mixture and whip briskly, then pour into a buttered 2-quart mold. Pour 2 cups of water into the slow cooker, place the mold on a rack or trivet in the cooker, cover the pot, and cook on High for 2 to 3 hours. Serve warm with cream.
Makes 8 servings.

No-Egg Rice Pudding
4 to 6 hours

Madame Bertrand, my landlady in southern France, made rice pudding this way.

1 cup raw converted rice
2½ cups milk
⅔ cup granulated sugar
½ cup golden seedless raisins
½ tsp. salt
½ tsp. nutmeg
Rind of half a lemon, slivered
½ tsp. vanilla
½ cup chilled heavy cream or half-and-half

To Cook: Place all the ingredients except the cream in the slow cooker and stir once. Cover and cook on Low for 4 to 6 hours. Serve lukewarm with chilled heavy cream or half-and-half.
Makes 8 to 10 servings.

Rice Pudding with Bourbon
4 to 6 hours

I make this with leftover rice, but you can start from scratch by cooking ½ cup raw rice as directed on the package.

3½ cups milk
1 cup cooked white rice
3 eggs, slightly beaten
⅓ cup granulated sugar
2 tsp. vanilla
½ cup golden seedless raisins
1½ tsp. grated lemon rind
1 tsp. nutmeg
2 Tbs. butter
3 Tbs. bourbon or dark rum
½ cup sweetened whipped cream

To Cook: Warm the milk and pour it over the rice. Into the eggs, beat the sugar, vanilla, raisins, and lemon rind. Stir the milk and rice into the egg mixture. Scrape into the slow cooker. Sprinkle with nutmeg and dot with butter. Cover and cook on Low for 4 to 6 hours. Turn into a serving bowl and stir in the bourbon. Serve the pudding lukewarm with a dollop of sweetened whipped cream on top.
Makes 6 to 8 servings.

Baked Stuffed Apples
3 to 5 hours

Following the method described below, you can bake apples plain. Stuffed as in this recipe, they make a real party dessert. If you bake them plain, put a little sugar and ¼ cup of water in the slow cooker.

6 medium tart red apples
1 cup light brown sugar
¼ cup golden seedless raisins
1 Tbs. orange rind
¼ cup soft butter
2 cups very hot water
3 Tbs. orange juice concentrate

To Cook: Wash, core, and stem the apples, but don't peel them. Stand them in a buttered mold and stuff them with ⅔ cup of the brown sugar, the raisins, and the orange rind. Fill the tops of the core cavities with butter and sprinkle the remaining sugar over the tops. Place the mold in the slow cooker and pour 2 cups of hot water into the cooker. Sprinkle the orange juice concentrate over the apples, cover the cooker, and cook on Low for 3 to 5 hours or until the apples are tender.
Makes 6 servings.

Mother's Applesauce Recipe
6 to 8 hours

8 to 10 medium tart apples, peeled, cored, and sliced
½ cup water
½ cup sugar
½ tsp. salt
½ tsp. cinnamon
1 tsp. vanilla
2 Tbs. butter

To Cook: Place the apples in the slow cooker along with the water, sugar, salt, and cinnamon. Cover and cook on Low for 6 to 8 hours. Remove the cover, turn the heat off, and stir in the vanilla and the butter. Serve warm or chill before serving.
Makes 6 to 8 servings.

Papa's Applesauce Recipe
6 to 8 hours

8 to 10 medium tart   ½ cup sugar
   apples, peeled,   1 Tbs. grated orange
   cored, and sliced   rind
½ cup orange juice

To Cook: Place all the ingredients in the slow cooker, cover, and cook on Low for 6 to 8 hours.
Makes 6 to 8 servings.

Stewed Rhubarb
6 to 8 hours

4 cups 2-inch pieces   ½ cup water
   rhubarb   2 Tbs. butter
½ to ¾ cup sugar   ½ tsp. vanilla

To Cook: Place the rhubarb in the slow cooker along with the sugar and water. Cover and cook on Low for 6 to 8 hours. Remove the cover, turn off the heat, and stir in the butter and the vanilla. Chill before serving.
Makes 6 to 8 servings.

Quick Rhubarb Mousse
6 to 8 hours

4 cups 2-inch pieces   ½ tsp. vanilla
   rhubarb   1 pint unsweetened
½ to ¾ cup sugar   heavy cream,
½ cup water   whipped
2 Tbs. butter

To Cook: Place the rhubarb in the slow cooker along with the sugar and water. Cover and cook on Low for 6 to 8 hours. Remove the cover, turn off the heat, and stir in the butter and the vanilla. Drain away most of the juice. Fold the strained rhubarb into the unsweetened heavy cream, whipped. Turn into a serving bowl, cover, and chill for a few minutes in the freezer before serving.
Makes 8 to 10 servings.

Compote of Dried Fruit
10 to 12 hours

For special occasions, serve this with bourbon-flavored whipped cream.

1 cup dried prunes   2½ cups water
1 cup dried golden   Slivered rind of ¼
   seedless raisins   lemon
1 cup dried apricots

To Cook: Place all the ingredients in the slow cooker, cover, and cook on Low for 10 to 12 hours or overnight. Chill before serving.
Makes 8 to 10 servings.

Stewed Prunes
10 to 12 hours

Do these overnight. They make a great breakfast served warm with cream and toasted, buttered whole wheat bread.

1 lb. dried prunes   Rind of ¼ lemon
4 cups water   ½ tsp. vanilla

To Cook: Place everything but the vanilla in the slow cooker, cover, and cook on Low for 10 to 12 hours or overnight. Remove the cover, turn off the heat, and add the vanilla. Turn into a serving bowl and allow to cool to lukewarm before serving.
Makes 6 to 8 servings.

Fresh Fruit Compote
5 to 7 hours

This is a basic recipe for cooking fresh fruits in the slow cooker. Use it to make compote of pears, apples, cherries, peaches, plums, nectarines, or apricots. You can make compotes of mixed fresh fruits or of a single fruit. Use compote of pears and peaches to make classic desserts such as Poires Hélène and Peach Melba (page 95).

2 cups water   Rind of ¼ lemon
1 cup sugar   ½ tsp. vanilla
¼ tsp. salt
5 cups fresh fruit,
   peeled, halved or
   quartered

To Cook: Place all the ingredients except the vanilla in the slow cooker, cover, and cook on Low for 5 to 7 hours. Remove the cover, stir in the vanilla, and then chill the fruit.
Makes 6 to 8 servings.

Poires Hélène

This is a classic dessert from the turn of the century. To make it, you need prepared chocolate sauce.

8 scoops vanilla ice   ¾ cup chocolate
   cream   sauce
8 pears cooked as for
   Fresh Fruit Com-
   pote (page 94)

Before Serving: In each fruit cup, place the vanilla ice cream with two pear halves on top and drizzle with chocolate sauce.
Makes 8 servings.

Peach Melba

For this classic dessert, you need fresh raspberries.

2 cups raspberries   4 peaches, cooked as
Sugar to taste   for Fresh Fruit
1 Tbs. Kirsch liqueur   Compote (page 94)
                    1 quart vanilla ice
                      cream

Before Serving: Wash and hull the raspberries and puree in a blender on low speed, adding a little sugar at a time. Do not make the berries overly sweet. Stir in the Kirsch liqueur and chill for several hours. Place the ice cream in a serving bowl in scoops and set the peach halves on top. Cover with raspberry puree and serve.
Makes 8 servings.

Homemade Mincemeat
16 to 20 hours

This takes 16 to 20 hours of cooking time, and without a slow cooker it's a chore. First the meat is cooked for 8 to 10 hours, then the mincemeat is put together and cooked an additional 8 to 10 hours. If you don't have a food chopper, you can try to blend the ingredients in your blender, but it's tiresome. However, it's fun to try once, and homemade mincemeat is both economical and awfully good in pies and tarts. Put it up in jars and give it at Christmas.

1 lb. lean chuck   1 Tbs. ground nut-
   beef, cut into   meg
   1-inch cubes   2 cups granulated
2 to 3 cups water   sugar
2 lb. tart apples,   1 cup apple cider
   pared and diced   1 Tbs. ground
2⅔ cups seedless   cloves
   raisins   1 Tbs. ground
2½ cups currants   cinnamon
¼ lb. citron   ¼ lb. ground beef
2 tsp. salt   suet

To Cook: Place the meat in the slow-cook pot with enough water to cover. Cover the pot and cook on Low for 8 to 10 hours, or until very tender. Turn off the heat. Remove the meat from the pot, but leave 1 cup of the broth in the pot. Put the meat through a food chopper and mix with the apples, raisins, currants, and citron. Add this and all the other ingredients to the broth in the slow cooker. Stir well, cover, and cook on Low for 8 to 10 hours more. Spoon into clean, dry, canning jars, seal, and process in a boiling-water bath. Or refrigerate.
Makes enough for 4 pies.

Apple Butter
11 to 13 hours

The big advantage in making preserve butters in a slow cooker is that you don't have to stir or stand over the pot waiting to stir. Adapt your favorite fruit butter recipes to fit the instructions and cooking time.

2 quarts sweet cider   ¼ tsp. cinnamon
4 lb. sweet but tart   ¼ tsp. allspice
   apples, peeled,   ⅛ tsp. ground cloves
   cored, and sliced   1 tsp. salt
About 3 cups granu-
   lated sugar

To Cook: Place the cider and the apples in the slow cooker. Cover and cook on Low for 10 to 12 hours; do not stir. Rub the apples through a sieve; measure the apples and add as much sugar as there is apple. Add the spices and salt and return to the cooker. Cover, and cook on Low for another hour. Pour into clean, dry, ½-pint canning jars. Seal and process in a boiling-water bath or store in refrigerator.
Makes 4 to 5 pints.

Index

Apple Butter, 95
Applesauce, 93-94

Baked Beans, 44, 75, 78
Baked Stuffed Apples, 93
Baking, 82-85
Barbecue, 24
Bavarian Pork, 42
Beans/bean dishes, 44, 75-76, 80
Beef à l'Estouffade, 26
Beef Shank, 34-35
Blanquette de Veau, 39
Boeuf Bourguignon, 30
Bolliti Misti, 29
Bones, 24, 56, 60
Boston Brown Bread, 90
Bouillon, 10, 56, 60, 63
Breads, 57, 86-90
Breakfast, 12, 79-80, 85
Brisket, marinated, 34

Cakes, 87, 90-92
Carbonnades à la Flamande, 31
Casseroles, 70-74, 77-80
Cassoulet, 44
Cereals, 12, 76, 85
Chicken à la King, 47
Chicken Cacciatore, 48
Chicken Pot Pie, 46-47
Chicken Wings Marcel, 48-49
Chicken with Beans, 46
Chicken with Celery, 46
Chili con Carne, 38-39
Chowder, Clam, 68
Chowder, Corn, 67
Cocido, 36
Compotes, 85, 94
Coq au Vin, 49
Corn Bread, 90
Corned Beef, 53
Cornmeal Mush, 90
Curries, 28, 40, 43, 50
Custards, 85, 92

Desserts, 85, 87, 90-95
Dried Foods, 10, 75-76, 94
Dutch Ovens, 7-8, 82

Fish, 10, 61-62
Fruits, 73, 85, 93-95

Grains, 12, 75, 79-80
Gravies, 10, 56, 82
Gremolata Sauce, 40

Hamburger, 23, 38
Ham in Cider, 43
Ham Roll, 44
Heart, Beef, 52-53

Irish Stew, 22, 49, 51-52

Lamb Omar Khayyam, 50-51
Lentils, 76, 78-79

Meatballs, 38
Meat Loaf, 37
Meat Pies, 12, 32-33, 46
Meats, 22-53
  Beef, 24-39
  Ham, 41, 43-44, 60
  Lamb, 49-52
  Mutton, 49
  Pork, 41-42, 44
  Veal, 39-40
Meat Sauce, 36-37, 78
Meat Stock, 10, 22, 56, 60
Mincemeat, 95
Moussaka, 50
Muffins, 12, 82, 88

Navarin Printanier, 52
New England Boiled Dinner, 41, 42-43

Osso Bucco, 40

Pastas, 76-77
Paupiettes de Boeuf, 25
Peach Melba, 95
Poires Hélène, 95
Polenta, 75, 78
Pork Chops, 42
Pot au Feu, 28
Puddings, 70, 77, 85, 91, 92-93
Purees, 76, 79

Ratatouille, 70, 71
Red Beef Appetizer, 24
Red Cooked Chicken, 46
Rice/rice dishes, 10, 38, 66, 76, 77
Roasts, 14, 23, 26, 28, 34
Roux, 9

Sausages, 41
  Polish, 41, 53
Short Ribs, 34
Slow-Pot Cooking, 7-12, 22-24, 55-57, 61, 70-71, 75-76, 82-85
  Care of Cooker, 13-20
  Timing, 13-14, 18, 22-23
Soups, 10, 55-68
  Baked Bean, 61, 68
  Beans and Ham, 65
  Beef and Cabbage, 61, 64
  Beef Gumbo, 61, 64
  Bouillabaisse, 61, 62
  Carrot, 58
  Chicken, 58, 66
  Curry, 65
  Dutch with Bread, 57
  Egg Drop, 61, 66
  Leek, 61, 62
  Lentil, 60
  Onion, 58-59
  Parsley, 59
  Scotch Broth, 61, 67
  Split-Pea, 60
  Vegetable, 61, 66-67
  Vichyssoise, 55, 62-63
Southern Ham Pot, 44
Steaks, 23, 24, 25-26, 33, 35
Stewed Prunes, 94
Stews, 14, 22, 29, 30-31, 51-52, 62
Stuffed Beef Heart, 52-53
Stuffed Cabbage Catalan, 41, 43
Stuffed Cabbage Rolls, 72
Swiss Steak Jardinière, 33

Tongue, Smoked, 53

Vegetable, Marmite, 73
Vegetables, 22, 70-73, 75
  Cabbage, 41, 43, 70, 72, 73
  Carrots, 70, 74
  Celery, 45, 46
  Eggplants, 50
  Peppers, 70, 72
  Potatoes, 71, 73, 74
  Rhubarb, 94
  Tomatoes, 39, 70, 71
  Turnips, 70, 74
  Zucchini, 30